CAREERS IN FILM AND TELEVISION

SO YOU WANT TO WORK IN ANIMATION & SPECIAL EFFECTS?

Torene Svitil

Enslow Publishers, Inc.
40 Industrial Road
Box 398
Berkeley Heights, NJ 07922
USA

http://www.enslow.com

Library of Congress Cataloging-in-Publication Data

Svitil, Torene.
    So you want to work in animation & special effects? / Torene Svitil.
        p. cm. — (Careers in film and television)
    Includes bibliographical references and index.
    ISBN-13: 978-0-7660-2737-4
    ISBN-10: 0-7660-2737-6
    1. Animation (Cinematography)—Vocational guidance. 2. Cinematography—Special
    effects—Vocational guidance. I. Title. II. Series.
    TR897.5.S85 2007
    778.5'2345023—dc22

                                                          2006009734

Printed in the United States of America

10 9 8 7 6 5 4 3 2 1

To Our Readers:
We have done our best to make sure all Internet addresses in this book were active and
appropriate when we went to press. However, the author and the publisher have no control over
and assume no liability for the material available on those Internet sites or on other Web
sites they may link to. Any comments or suggestions can be sent by e-mail to
comments@enslow.com or to the address on the back cover.

Illustration Credits: All interior images courtesy of the Everett Collection, Inc.

Cover Illustration: Enslow Publishers, Inc./iStockphoto Inc./Jupiterimages
Corporation.

CONTENTS

INTRODUCTION

At any given moment on any given day, someone is watching a moving image somewhere in the world. Whether in their neighborhood theaters, or in the comfort of their own home, people love to watch movies. According to recent statistical studies, watching TV and DVDs is America's number one favorite leisure activity. The true mass media, movies and TV appeal to all ages and types, especially young people. Ninety percent of America's teens report going to the movies at least occasionally, and over sixty percent say they watch a DVD at least once a week.

The impact of movies and television on our lives is immeasurable. More than books, magazines, newspapers, and the Internet, moving images influence the way we think and feel about the world. We use them to explain events and define attitudes. They are our favorite points of reference.

In addition to their ability to reflect and interpret reality, movies are an ideal vehicle for the imagination. Although many people think of animation only in terms of cartoons, it is

ANIMATION—The process of photographing models, puppets, pictures, or artwork one frame at a time. Between each frame, some aspect of the subject is altered so that when the film is projected, the subject appears to move.

4

one of the most versatile tools in the filmmaker's kit. Animation allows filmmakers to put on the screen anything they can conceive of, whether its techniques are used to create an entirely animated movie or, as visual effects, to generate otherworldly landscapes or fantastic creatures.

This book in the *Careers in Film and Television* series focuses on the art of animation and visual effects. All movies, whether live action (film of real people and things) or animation, consist of a rapidly moving series of still pictures. Each still image in a movie is called a frame.

Movies are projected at twenty-four frames a second. That means it takes twenty-four frames of film to

> FRAME—A single image on a film strip.

make one second on screen. In live action films, the camera runs at a constant speed, but each frame of an animated film is created separately, one at a time.

There are many different ways of animating pictures, including drawing and posing objects, but they all depend on a phenomenon called persistence of vision.

> PERSISTENCE OF VISION—
> The illusion of movement created when a series of still pictures flashes by in rapid succession.

When people see a series of images flashing quickly by, they cannot separate them into individual pictures, so the brain is fooled into believing the images are moving. This is persistence of vision, and it makes television and movies possible.

Animation was first used to play sight tricks on the audience. In the 1890s, French magician George

STOP-MOTION—
A method of animating models by physically altering their position in between the photography of each frame.

ROTOSCOPE—A method of projecting live action footage so that it can be traced frame by frame by an animator.

CHARACTER ANIMATION—
Animation that reveals a character's personality by the way it moves and behaves.

Méliès made objects appear to turn into people or different objects using stop-motion photography, a method of animating objects by moving them slightly between each frame. By the early twentieth century, animators such as J. Stuart Blackton and Winsor McCay were making animated films composed entirely of drawings. The rotoscope, a technique patented in 1917 by Max Fleischer, allowed animators to create lifelike animation by tracing a projected film of an actor frame by frame.

Early in the twentieth century, comic strip artist Winsor McCay changed the way animated films were drawn. While making his 1914 film *Gertie the Dinosaur,* McCay discovered that if he drew on transparent paper, background drawings could be easily traced. Now that he did not have to redraw the background for every scene, he had time to focus on animating characters.

McCay gave "Gertie" easy-to-read expressions and slow, shy movements, which created an impression of a likeable, somewhat goofy dinosaur. By using Gertie's actions to reveal her personality, McCay laid the foundation of what is called character animation. Character animation, used for most

Gertie the Dinosaur, in an animated short first released in 1914.

cartoons, reveals a character's personality by making it move and react in specific ways.

In 1914, Earl Hurd discovered that if he drew on clear sheets of celluloid (similar to photographic film), called cels, he could layer his drawings under the animation camera. The number of cels depended on the number of moving parts in each scene. Animators only had to make a new cel when one of the parts, for example, the character's hand, changed position. Cels soon became the standard for producing hand-drawn animated films.

The first cartoon series, *Colonel Heeza Liar's African Hunt*, debuted in 1914. Walt Disney's series *Alice in Cartoonland*, which began in 1923, featured a live child actress in animated surroundings, similar to *Who Framed Roger Rabbit*? The cartoon character "Felix the Cat" was so popular in the 1920s that toys and other objects with his image were produced.

CEL—A transparent sheet of plastic used in hand-drawn animation.

CEL ANIMATION—The traditional method of creating hand-drawn two-dimensional animation. Each frame is drawn and painted on a clear acetate cel. This cel is placed on top of a painted background and then photographed.

The addition of sound and music made animation more popular and more "life-like." Although it wasn't the first sound cartoon, *Steamboat Willie* (1928), which marked Mickey Mouse's debut, was the first to use synchronized music and sound effects. Mickey Mouse cartoons became so popular that they were often advertised over the feature and were considered great drawing cards.

By the end of the silent era, animation had become an industry with trained artists with an audience eager for their product. Advances and refinements in the business of character animation continued to be made during the 1930s and 1940s, especially at the Walt Disney studios. Other artists experimented with animating everything from sand to clay to paper silhouettes to puppets to live action.

The development of computer animation resulted

8

A colorized still from the 1928 animated short Steamboat Willie, *which introduced the famous Disney character Mickey Mouse.*

in animated films like *Shrek* and *The Incredibles*, as well as the ground-breaking visual effects of *The Matrix* films and *The Lord of the Rings* trilogy.

Today, many animated and live action films are at least partly made with the help of a computer, but the basis of all animation and visual effects is the principles and techniques that were developed in the early days of traditional animation.

1

CREATING MOVEMENT

In a lecture he gave at the computer graphics conference SIGGRAPH (Special Interest Group for Computer Graphics), Oscar-winning animator and Pixar executive John Lasseter (*Toy Story, Finding Nemo*) explained the appeal of his computer-animated films.

> When I presented the first animation I had created with a computer . . . a number of people asked me what cool new software I had used to achieve such believable characters. . . . It was not the software that gave life to the characters, it was these principles of animation, these tricks of the trade that animators had developed over fifty years ago.[1]

As Lasseter suggests, animation is a collection of tricks that fool the eye and brain into believing that lines and volumes on a movie screen are characters with lives, personalities, and emotions, or are settings that really exist. Even realistic-looking computer animation depends on these techniques to develop credible characters and surroundings. The same techniques and skills help viewers accept unnatural worlds and events like those in *Batman Begins* and *War of the Worlds*. Once these principles are learned, animators have a solid basis for experimentation in any medium or style.

The best model for believable animation is real life. "There is no doubt when a dog is ashamed, or proud, or playful, or sad (or belligerent, sleepy, disgusted, indignant). He speaks with his whole body in both attitude and movement," explain Disney animators Frank Thomas and Ollie Johnston.[2]

Animated characters, like human actors, express themselves with gestures, mannerisms, posture, and facial expressions, as well as voice. A tilted head indicates surprise. A body leaning forward suggests speed. An animator's job is to bring graphic images to life through movement. An animator's ability to create believable gestures and movements is what is meant by "acting" in animated films.[3]

Most animators have a mirror at their desk so they can study themselves making the expression they are trying to animate. While working on *Bambi*, Disney animators watched the dissection of a fawn's corpse to learn the way its muscles and bones worked together. Later, a pair of live fawns were kept in a pen near the animation building where the animators could observe them.[4] Similarly, John Lasseter insisted that the team animating *Finding Nemo* learn scuba diving so they really knew what the light, plants, and water looked like in a coral reef.

SQUASH AND STRETCH

According to Frank Thomas and Ollie Johnston, squash and stretch is the most important technique for animators to master.[5] Squash and stretch is used to animate everything from walking and running to dialogue and facial expressions. The technique makes animated movement look realistic. In the squashed position a form is flattened out or pushed together and is completely extended in the stretched position.

Seen in slow motion, a bouncing ball stretches as it gets closer to the ground, flattens when it lands and lengthens again on the way back up. When Wile E. Coyote falls off a cliff in Road Runner cartoons, his body smashes into the ground (squash) and then elongates into a bounce (stretch).

SQUASH AND STRETCH—Extreme positions in an animated movement. Squash and stretch can be exaggerated for comic effect.

Muscles will contract and extend no matter how small the movement. When people smile, their cheeks bulge, narrowing their eyes, and shortening the face (squash). As the smile is relaxed, the cheeks drop away from the eyes and the whole face gets slightly longer (stretch). The improvement made by squash and stretch can be seen in Mickey Mouse cartoons. In the early cartoons, before animators started to use squash and stretch, Mickey had a hard round head. Later, squash and stretch gave him flexible cheeks that moved when he talked or chewed, and he acquired more personality.

Squash and stretch is more exaggerated in comedies like the Road Runner cartoons and more subtle in a drama or in characters, like Snow White, who are not primarily comic. When the wolf in a Tex Avery cartoon gets a look at beautiful Red Hot Riding Hood, his eyeballs almost leap from his head.

14

Snow White's gestures, by contrast, are more natural.

The principle of squash and stretch also applies to visual effects. When the clones in *The Matrix* are punched or kicked, their bodies squash under the impact and then spring back as if nothing had happened. *Spider-Man*'s computer-animated stunt double lands in a crouch after he jumps from a height, just as a real person would. Digital backgrounds, those that are created in the computer, react to the weather, to gravity, and to other forces. Digital trees will bend in a heavy wind, for example.

Keanu Reeves clashes with Hugo Weaving in a high-end special effects battle from **The Matrix** *(1999).*

SHAPE

Shape helps define a character's personality. Cute characters, like the animals in *Bambi*, will have features similar to a baby's, such as a large head, small body, high forehead, big eyes, and short, plump arms and legs. A villainous character could have a small head, a thick or nonexistent neck, and a big chest. Comic characters have exaggerated features.

> DIGITAL—Recording, storing, and transmitting images, sounds, and data in the computer in combinations of ones and zeros. Digital information can be copied and transmitted repeatedly with no loss of detail.

Animators can also use shape to play against stereotypes. In *Shrek 2*, handsome Prince Charming, the physical epitome of a cartoon hero, is self-centered and foolish, while big, ugly Shrek has the looks of a monster but the kind heart and bravery of a hero.

APPEAL

To an animator, appeal is anything that an audience likes to see. Even villains need appeal, or the audience will not want to watch what they are doing. It helps if the character has a personality that the audience can identify with, although it does not have to be a particularly likeable personality. Syndrome, the villain in *The Incredibles* is not likeable, but most people know someone who, like Syndrome, wants to get back at the person he imagines has insulted him.

In his autobiography, animator Chuck Jones explains that he gave even his most caricatured cartoon characters recognizable human traits. "Bugs Bunny is simply, and only, trying to remain alive in a world of predators . . . Daffy Duck is simply trying to get ahead; Pepé Le Pew is simply trying to get a girl . . . Wile E. Coyote and Sylvester are simply trying to get something to eat."[6]

These human qualities help viewers understand and laugh at the actions of a rabbit, a duck, a skunk, a coyote, and a cat. In creating his characters, Jones says: "I don't want something that's realistic. I want something that's believable."[7]

The difference between realistic and believable can be seen in the design of the fish in *Finding Nemo*. Although the colors and shapes of the fish are taken from life, the animators gave them eyes in the front of their heads, eyelids, and eyebrows, humanistic features that real fish don't have, so that their faces could express recognizable emotions.

MOVEMENT

Movement and character are closely connected, as Winsor McCay discovered. Donald Duck does not behave or move like a real duck, but his physical behavior is believable and reveals his quick-tempered, egotistical personality. Dick Lundy, one of Donald's animators, describes how Donald reacts when he gets mad. "I had him lean forward, chin out, arm straight out and fisted. The other arm, with fist, was swinging back and forth. His one foot was out straight, heel on floor, the other foot under him as he hopped up and down, quacking."[8]

ACTION

Animators agree that all movements should exist for a reason. By considering the reasons behind the actions, they will not seem random but will tell a story.

A woman mailing a bill will act differently from one sending a letter to a man she loves. The woman mailing a bill would probably toss it quickly into the mailbox. If she was broke, however, she might hesitate, wondering if she should wait to pay the bill until she has more money. A woman in love might kiss her letter or hold it close to her heart. Knowing the reason behind the behavior, the animator can create more interesting scenes and more complex characters.

Animation supervisor Randall William Cook (*The Lord of the Rings*) describes how animators gave Gollum the appearance of intelligence: "In shots where Gollum had no dialogue, the animators would write out precisely what [he] was thinking on every frame. . . . We had to fool the lie detector of the movie camera into believing Gollum was really thinking, not pulling faces."[9]

No two characters perform the same action in the same way. In Jan Pinkava's computer animated short, *Geri's Game*, an old man plays chess against himself. His personality changes depending on whether he is playing the black or the white chessmen. First seen hunched over the chessboard, the man's movements are small and tentative. When he takes the part of his imagined opponent, however, he sits upright and makes expansive, large gestures.

SECONDARY ACTION

Secondary actions follow a character's main action. Just as a live-action actor uses small gestures to

A scene from Shrek 2, *released in 2004. The animated feature was one of the most profitable film sequels in box office history.*

round out a characterization, a secondary action adds another element to the scene. In *Shrek 2*, Princess Fiona catches a mermaid kissing Shrek and throws her back into the sea (main action). Afterward, she dusts her hands against each other (secondary action) with a look of satisfaction on her face. Her gesture—and Shrek's reaction to it—makes a potentially cruel action seem funny.

ANTICIPATION, FOLLOW THROUGH, AND OVERLAPPING ACTION

If a character's actions begin and stop abruptly, viewers will have a hard time understanding what is happening in the scene, and the actions will look unnatural. Anticipation, follow through, and overlapping action describe some of the ways animators handle those problems. Combined with squash and stretch and timing, these techniques create an illusion of weight and believability.

Anticipation shows viewers what is going to happen. Consider a pitcher on the mound. As he prepares to hurl the ball, his body draws backward. This is anticipation. During any action, different parts of the body move at different times. When a bearded man turns his head, for example, his beard follows

> **SECONDARY ACTION**—An action that takes place after a character's main action.

> **ANTICIPATION**—An animation technique in which a character indicates a major action before it begins.

slightly later. This is called overlapping action. Back on the mound, the pitcher raises one leg and brings his arm back behind him.

Now, he throws. First his body leans forward, followed by his arm and then the ball. After releasing the ball the pitcher's arm follows the ball for a moment, and his body leans further forward. This is follow through.

> OVERLAPPING ACTION—In animating figures and objects, different parts of the animation move separately from each other.

In a comedy, all these moves are exaggerated. In a humorous version of the above scene, the pitcher leans so far back he almost falls. His windup lasts several seconds, and its momentum will pull him forward. His jersey billows

> FOLLOW THROUGH— The extension and continuation of an animated action.

and flaps as he flings the ball, and his body twists into a knot after the release.

TIMING

Timing is the length of time an action takes on screen. The length is determined by the number of drawings used from the beginning of the action to its end. The beginning and ending drawing in an action are called extremes or key poses. Extremes are made for each major change in the character's action, for example, a change in the direction the character is moving. The most squashed or the most

TIMING—The number of drawings it takes to complete an action. The more drawings, the longer the action lasts on screen and the smoother the action appears.

stretched position of an action is an extreme. In computer animation, extremes are called key frames.

Animators practice extremes by drawing a bouncing ball. The first extreme is the top position, when the ball is released. The ball touching the ground would be the second extreme. The third extreme would be drawn when the ball reaches the top position again, and so on.

Once the extremes are set, an animator adds other drawings called in-betweens, to show the progress of the action and link all the drawings together. An action's smoothness and speed depend on the number of in-betweens created for the sequence. The more drawings used to complete an action, the longer that action lasts on screen, and the smoother the action will look.

EXTREMES—The beginning and ending drawings of an animated movement.

KEY DRAWINGS—The drawings that indicate story points or major changes, or that tell what is happening in the scene. In computer generated animation they are called key frames.

Any comedian will admit that it is timing as much as dialogue that makes a joke work. To be effective, timing should vary from scene to scene. Relentless fast action can be tiring rather than funny. Constantly slow action risks putting viewers to sleep.

Chuck Jones's Wile E. Coyote is famous for plunging off cliffs in his pursuit of the Road Runner. Timing is crucial to the humor of these scenes. There is a moment when the coyote realizes he is suspended in air. He feels around with his paw. Nothing. He feels again. Nothing. Then suddenly, as if his realization is causing his fall, he plunges to the ground. Jones explains: "I found that if the coyote fell off a cliff it would take eighteen frames for him to disappear, then fourteen frames later, he would hit. It seemed to me that thirteen frames didn't work in terms of humor and neither did fifteen frames; fourteen frames got a laugh."[10]

> **IN-BETWEENS—**
> The stages of action between key frames.

Timing focuses attention where the story requires it. John Lasseter's computer-animated short film *Luxo Jr.*, is about the relationship between two desk lamps, a father and a son. Because there is no dialogue, the entire story is told through the characters' movements. According to Lasseter, the action had to be timed so that only one character had an important action at any one time. At first "Dad" is on-screen alone. "As soon as Jr. hops onscreen, he is moving faster than Dad; therefore the audience's eye immediately goes to him and stays there."[11]

Timing is also used to demonstrate how big or how heavy objects and characters are. Heavy objects take time and effort to start, stop, or change movements, while light objects are easier to set in

The special effects work that brought the character of Gollum (from The Lord of the Rings *trilogy) to life marked a tremendous leap forward in effects technology.*

motion. A light tap sends a balloon shooting away, but it takes a lot of muscle to move a boulder.

STORYBOARDS

Every second of a typical animated film involves twelve to twenty-four different drawings. That comes to over 50,000 visuals for a seventy-minute film. Because it is expensive and time-consuming to complete an animated sequence, each step is worked out beforehand on a storyboard.

Storyboards look something like an elaborate comic strip or graphic novel. They are made up of quick sketches, small drawings, and captions and may include bits of dialogue.

> STORYBOARD—A device, similar to a comic strip or graphic novel, that is used to plan animated films of any type.

Although traditional animators usually display storyboard drawings on the wall, computer animators either scan their drawings into the computer or draw directly in the computer.

Animators use storyboards to experiment with different versions of characters and background. They are used to plan camera moves such as long shots and close-ups and to determine where special effects or sound effects are needed. Using storyboards, animators can pinpoint any potential problems, determine the key moments of

> LONG SHOT— Describes a film shot when a character or object is shown at a distance and appears small in the frame.

the story, and set the order of sequences. They are revised often as details of the story or the progression of the images is worked out.

COLOR, PERSPECTIVE, AND SOUND

Color supports the story and establishes mood. Warm colors suggest an active or aggressive atmosphere. Cool colors are usually perceived as peaceful or quiet. Bright colors are cheerful. The two

CLOSE UP—When a character or object is drawn or photographed from a short distance. In a close up, the subject of the shot will fill most of the frame.

different behaviors of the old man in *Geri's Game* are subliminally emphasized by placing fading yellow leaves behind the quieter personality and brilliant red leaves behind the more aggressive personality.

At the beginning of *The Incredibles*, during the golden age of superheroes, the colors are very bright and intense. When Mr. Incredible is shown working at his boring job for an insurance company, the colors are muted and lifeless. Finally, during the big fight scene at the end of the film, when the Incredibles are able to use their powers again, the colors of the costumes and the backgrounds are dazzling.

Perspective, a drawing technique in which two apparently parallel lines come together at a point, is used to create an illusion of depth and distance. In animation, it shows the relationship between characters and background. Characters who are farther away will be smaller than characters who are nearby. As objects in the background become smaller along the invisible converging lines, the background looks deeper and more three-dimensional.

Although animation can be totally silent, music, dialogue, narration, and sound effects add another level of interest and believability to animation. Creepy sounds make a spooky scene scarier. Cheerful music combined with scary drawings cues the audience that the scene is meant to be humorous.

Sound and sound effects such as a dog barking in the background, the whoosh of traffic, ringing telephones, or wind in the trees make animation and visual effects seem more real and add to the effectiveness of the scene.

> PERSPECTIVE—A technique in drawing and painting in which parallel lines are represented as converging so as to give the illusion of depth and distance.

Images are also inspired by sounds. Sound tracks for animated films are recorded before any images are drawn. As they begin to animate characters, animators listen to the vocal track over and over. They try to match the character's expression and mouth movements to the voice actors' inflections. The look of a character can also be inspired by an actor's voice. An actor with a deep voice might motivate an animator to create a large, powerful-looking character, for example.

Disney's 1940 film *Fantasia* demonstrates the connection between music and animation. Each musical sequence in the film has a different composer, mood, and animation style. Amilcare Ponchielli's lighthearted *The Dance of the Hours* inspired a parody of classical ballet, starring hippos, elephants, ostriches, and alligators. Abstract shapes moved in rhythm with Johan Sebastian Bach's cerebral *Toccata and Fugue in D Minor.* Modest

Disney's Fantasia *(1940) set a standard of quality in animation that would not be matched for decades.*

Mussorgsky's stirring *Night on Bald Mountain* evoked images with powerful, dramatic angles and dark colors.

The creation of the world was animated to Igor Stravinsky's *The Rite of Spring*. Art director Dick Kelsey composed a poem describing the difficulty of creating an effective mood while leaving the scene light enough for details to be visible:

> *The Rite of Spring* is a moody thing
> So make it dark as night
> With lots of jets and black silhouettes
> But be damn sure it's light[12]

Effective animation and visual effects never exploit an effect simply to show off. Every technique is used for a reason, as John Lasseter advises: "In every step of the production of your animation, the story, the design, the staging, the animation, the editing, the lighting, the sound, etc., ask yourself 'why?' Why is this here? Does it further the story? Does it support the whole?"[13]

2

TRADITIONAL CEL ANIMATION: TWO APPROACHES

Canadian animator Norman McLaren famously said: "Animation is not the art of drawings that move, but the art of movements that are drawn."[1] No one did more to advance this idea than Walt Disney.

It is no coincidence that most Americans associate animation with the recognizable Disney style. During animation's early years, almost every important advance in the field was developed at the Disney Studios. With Walt Disney's encouragement, his large staff of animators, filmmakers, businessmen, and technicians developed new ways of drawing characters. They also invented new equipment to create animated films that looked richer and more three-dimensional.

Disney animators established a standard that could not be ignored. Other animators either reacted against it or tried to copy it. "Of course we stole from Disney then," Warner Bros.' animation director Chuck Jones admitted. "*Everybody* stole from Disney then."[2]

Walt Disney was born in Chicago in 1901. He worked as a cartoonist and photographer for his high school magazine and studied at the Art Institute of Chicago. While employed by an advertising company, Walt and his friend Ub Iwerks began making animated films at night. Eventually, Walt convinced investors to finance a small studio called Laugh-O-Gram Films. The studio quickly went bankrupt when Walt failed to find distribution for any of their films. In California, where he had gone to join his brother Roy, Walt had some success with a series of films that featured a real girl named Alice (played by several different actresses during the series) in an animated cartoon setting.

In 1927, Walt and his staff developed a new cartoon character, Oswald the Rabbit. Later, Walt and Ub devised the character of Mickey Mouse. Ub drew Mickey, and Walt invented his personality and, for many years, supplied his voice.

INNOVATIONS

In *Steamboat Willie*, actions were coordinated with sound effects and music for the first time. Mickey Mouse, the cartoon's star, plays a cow's teeth like a xylophone, and cats meow when their tails are pulled. Disney animator Ward Kimball said: "You can have no idea of the impact that having these drawings suddenly speak and make noises had on audiences at that time. People went crazy over it."[3]

Shortly after *Steamboat Willie*, the studio released *The Skeleton Dance*, a mood piece set to music. Unlike traditional cartoons, the short focused on creating an eerie atmosphere rather than on telling a funny story. *The Skeleton Dance* was the first in the "Silly Symphonies" series, which, under the guidance of composer Carl Stalling, explored the connection between motion and sound.

Many early cartoons used very little dialogue and depended more on the kind of visual storytelling that was seen in silent movies. Even today, cartoons such as the Road Runner series and Pixar's animated short *For the Birds* (2000), rely on images rather than dialogue.

In 1932, the Technicolor cartoon *Flowers and Trees* won the Academy Award, the first ever for an animated short film. A few years later, in 1935, *The Tortoise and the Hare* made significant advances in creating the illusion of speed with animation.

Most cartoonists at this time were only interested in drawing well enough to make a joke work, but Disney animators developed real personalities for their characters. Walt pushed them to base their drawings in real life and to analyze the way humans

A black-and-white scene from one of Disney's earliest cartoons, Flowers and Trees *(1932).*

and animals moved. As he said, "The most hilarious comedy is always based on things actual."[4]

Disney started art classes for his animators. They also studied acting to learn how actors use expressions and behavior to convey emotions.[5] In 1933's *Three Little Pigs*, Disney animators developed distinctive personalities for each pig. Although the three pigs look alike, their personalities are defined by the way each one behaves. When Chuck Jones saw the film, he commented, "All we animators were dealing with after *Three Pigs* was acting."[6]

Storyboards, the animator's indispensable tool, originated at Disney in the 1930s.[7] Later, the pencil test was devised to let the filmmakers see how the animation might look before it was transferred to cels. A pencil test is simply a black and white film of the animators' pencil drawings. By adding movement to the drawings, the animators could see what was working and what needed improvement.

> **PENCIL TEST—**
> A film of animated sketches made to test animation before it is transferred to cels.

ECONOMICS

Walt Disney's emphasis on quality animation meant that his cartoons and movies were relatively expensive. To cut costs, he encouraged animators to simplify concepts, limit the number of characters, and find more economical ways of animating without sacrificing quality.

Disney animators discovered that it was difficult to keep angular shapes and lines consistent from drawing to drawing. They began to use rounded shapes when they drew characters, which were not only easier to animate but were also more appealing to viewers.

Some of the animators were terrific at working out movements and designing personality. To let them concentrate on what they did best, Walt developed a kind of assembly line. Lead animators turned over their rough drawings to assistants, who cleaned them up and filled in small details. Other artists would draw the in-betweens and backgrounds and plan the layout. This efficient system became standard procedure at all studios.[8]

THE MULTIPLANE CAMERA

Walt Disney was driven by the desire to give two-dimensional animation more depth, to look more three-dimensional. A major technological advance in this respect was the multiplane camera, which was first used in the 1937 film *The Old Mill*, a mood piece like *The Skeleton Dance*.

The multiplane camera had seven shelves or planes, which let animators place separate layers of artwork—for example a layer with characters, another of the near background and a third of the distant background—at different distances from the camera. When the camera focused on one level, the elements in front and behind were in soft focus, resulting in a picture with realistic-looking depth.

Cels could also be shifted from side to side, allowing certain elements, such as branches of overhanging trees, to be pulled slowly to the edge of the frame. This trick created an impression of a camera tracking through the scene, similar to camera moves in live action films. Although the multiplane camera produced unsurpassed effects, it was so expensive to operate that Disney was the only studio to use it regularly.[9]

THE FIRST AMERICAN FEATURE-LENGTH ANIMATED FILM

In 1937, when Walt Disney planned the studio's first feature-length animated film, *Snow White and the Seven Dwarfs*, animation was considered a medium for children. Feature-length animated films had been made as early as 1917, when Argentinean animator Quirino Cristiani made *The Apostle*.[10] German Lotte Reiniger made *The Adventures of Prince Ahmed* in 1926, using paper silhouettes and stop-motion photography. However, no one in the United States had attempted an animated feature. No one knew if children would sit still for a long animated film, or if such a film could be made interesting to adults.

Walt Disney believed that if the story and the look of the animation in *Snow White* were significantly different from those in short animated films, the movie would attract a large audience of both children and adults. He demanded characters as emotionally complex as human actors, along with sophisticated and beautiful animation.

As the studio started work on the film, the crew discovered that the pace of a feature-length film could not be as fast as that of a short. Walt told a reporter after the film was completed: "We started out . . . in the fast tempo that is the special technique of short subjects. But that wouldn't do; we soon realized there was danger of wearing out an audience. There was too much going on."[11]

When work on the movie was underway, the studio hired 300 new animators. Among the qualities they looked for were "good draftsmanship; knowledge of caricature, action, acting, the mechanics of animation, story structure and audience values; and an ability to think up and put over gags."[12] Before the movie was finished, over 750 additional animators were hired.[13]

Because the story of *Snow White* is based on a European fairy tale by the Grimm Brothers, Walt wanted the movie to have the look of an old European storybook. Delicate watercolor backgrounds were drawn by Swiss-born Albert Hurter and children's book illustrator Gustave Tenggren.

A model of the dwarfs' cottage was constructed from Hurter's sketches. Story sketch artists and layout artists used the model to figure out how characters would move through the set. To test lighting effects, the layout and background crew cut

Released in 1937, Disney Studio's first feature-length animated film, Snow White and the Seven Dwarfs, *was a ground-breaking film project.*

out little figures that would throw shadows on the walls and then shifted the lights to achieve the desired effect. The model helped animators work out better camera angles, interesting groupings of the characters, and better use of perspective.[14]

SPECIAL EFFECTS

During this film's production, Disney established the first animation special effects department. Special effects are anything in an animated film that moves and is not a character, including snow, water, rain, fire, smoke, falling leaves, and lightning.

One of the department's major achievements was devising a new way to draw shadows. Shadows help anchor animated characters in the background. Without them, animated characters can appear to float in space. Shadows also add depth and atmosphere to the settings. Before *Snow White*, shadows had been simply dark patches that followed the characters around. These opaque shadows blotted out every thing in their path, so no background detail could be drawn where a shadow might pass.

> **SPECIAL EFFECTS ANIMATION**—The animation of any moving object or substance other than the main characters, such as water, falling leaves, fire, smoke, clouds, and shadows. In live action films, effects like lightning, sparks, and smoke may be hand-drawn, painted, photographed, and composited optically or digitally.

For *Snow White*, special effects artists created more translucent shadows that allowed details of the background to be seen underneath. To do this they painted shadows on one cel. The cel with shadows was then layered with the character cels and exposed under the camera. The length of the exposure made the shadows lighter or darker.[15]

CHARACTERS

Snow White's characters presented another new set of design problems. According to Chuck Jones, cartoons featured animals because "it is easier and more believable to humanize animals than it is to humanize humans."[16] *Snow White* was the first Disney film that starred human characters instead of cute animals.

In addition to the characters of Snow White, the Wicked Queen, and the Prince, animators had to design seven believable and distinctive dwarfs, much like they did for *The Three Little Pigs*. Animator Bill Tytla explains: "If Doc would say something, they wouldn't all turn and look at him at the same time. Happy would probably be first, and Sleepy would probably be last in his reaction."[17]

Snow White and the Prince were more difficult to animate believably than the dwarfs because they were less caricatured. To help draw convincing poses for Snow White, the animators studied films of dancer Marge Belcher, who acted out Snow White's scenes for the camera.

Snow White was the first animated film to use the lyrics of songs to tell the audience something about the plot or the characters. *Snow White and the Seven Dwarfs'* combination of innovative animation with a carefully plotted story, catchy music, and engaging characters made it an enormous hit. At the time, no studio but Disney would undertake such an elaborate task. For many years, most feature animated films would be made by the Disney studio, each one an advance in technique over the previous film.

Max Fleischer was considered Walt Disney's main rival during the 1930s. Although best known for his invention of the rotoscope process, Fleischer, together with his brother Dave, developed a loose, rubbery, often surreal style of cartooning that differed significantly from Disney's moves toward realism. In the Fleischer cartoons, characters stretch and morph in time to music, rocks develop mouths, icicles sing, and ghosts reproduce by tearing off parts of themselves.

Fleischer's *Out of the Inkwell* series (1919–1929), featured a live action Max onscreen, who dipped his pen in an inkwell to bring Koko the Clown and other animated characters to life. In 1924, Koko starred in a sound cartoon, several years before Disney's *Steamboat Willie* was released. Fleischer's other innovations included "bouncing ball" sing-along Song Car-Tunes, the first use of in-betweeners, and the Three-Dimensional Setback, a small stage with animation cels hung in front, which created an effective three-dimensional effect when filmed.

> MORPHING—A process that makes one image appear to transform seamlessly into another.

Where Disney films were driven by story and character, Fleischer was more interested in bizarre visual and verbal gags. Rather than recording the sound track before animation began, sound in Fleischer cartoons was dubbed onto finished films with little concern for matching the characters' lip movements, and voice actors frequently improvised their dialogue.

Fleischer cartoons tended to be gritty and dark and focused on sex, death, and other adult concerns. The best-known Fleischer characters are sexy Betty Boop with her short skirts, garter, and little-girl voice, and the gruff, spinach-loving sailor Popeye. After the success of *Snow White and the Seven Dwarfs*, the Fleischers made two feature-length films, *Gulliver's Travels* (1939) and *Mr. Bug Goes to Town* (1941), which was later released as *Hoppity Goes to Town*. In 1942, Paramount Studios fired both of the brothers and renamed their studio Famous Studios.

TEX AVERY: FASTER IS FUNNIER

While Walt Disney was striving to make animation more artistic, Tex Avery just wanted to make people laugh. Frederick Ben Avery, later known as "Tex," was born in Taylor, Texas, in 1908. From an early age, Tex wanted to become a cartoonist. Failing to find work at local Dallas newspapers, he attended the Art Institute of Chicago for formal art training but left after a month. He again tried unsuccessfully for a cartooning job, this time with the Chicago papers, then moved to Los Angeles, where he was hired as an animation inker and painter and discovered a profession that suited him well.[18] Avery's irreverent attitude influenced cartoonists of the 1930s and 1940s such as Warner Bros.' Chuck Jones and Bob

Clampett and MGM's William Hanna and Joseph Barbera. His style of cartooning inspired *The Rocky and Bullwinkle Show* in the 1960s, the animated and live action film *Who Framed Roger Rabbit?*, the Genie sequence in *Aladdin*, and the television series *Ren & Stimpy* and *The Simpsons*, among many others. Like *The Simpsons*, the cartoons Avery directed parodied popular culture, including fairy tales, other movies, and other cartoons.

For Avery, the key to humor was surprise. His short, gag-packed cartoons are marked by surreal verbal and visual humor, exaggerated stretch and squash, and a solid understanding of comic timing. Unlike animators at Disney, who concentrated on story and character, Avery focused on getting as many jokes as possible into each short film.

"I started that faster trend," he declared. "We started filling in more gags. Prior to that they felt you had to have a story. Finally we got to where the 'story' was just a string of gags with a 'topper.' I found out the eye can register an action in five frames of film."[19]

A sequence in the 1943 MGM cartoon *Dumb-Hounded* illustrates Avery's rapid-fire pacing. The Wolf (one of Avery's favorite characters) has escaped from jail and is being tailed by Droopy, a bloodhound. In about twenty seconds, the Wolf dashes down a fire escape into a waiting cab, drives a scooter to a train that crosses the country, races a car to a ship that speeds across the ocean, bounces down the gangplank in a clanking jeep to a waiting airplane that zooms to the North Pole, where he gallops a horse to an isolated log cabin, only to find Droopy waiting. Avery then rewinds the escape, showing the Wolf retracing his route backwards in double-time.

At the same time that Walt Disney was trying to create what he called the "illusion of life" in his animated films, Avery was discovering that he could do anything he could imagine using animation.

In *Slap-Happy Lion*, a kangaroo hops into its own pocket and disappears. Characters run past the edge of the frame to reveal the sprocket holes at the film's edge, or they pause to address the audience or complain about their poor working conditions. If a film starts out in color, the characters might walk through the frame into a black-and-white world.

SPROCKET HOLES—
Small perforations along the edges of a film strip that hook on to the teeth of a sprocket wheel and move the film through a camera or projector.

In contrast to the wholesome, family-oriented Disney fare, Avery made sexy versions of fairy tales like Cinderella and Little Riding Hood. "We couldn't top Disney, and we knew he had the kid following, so we went for adults and young people," he said.[20] In a television documentary about the early Warner Bros. cartoons, Avery admitted: "I did things Disney wouldn't dare to do."[21]

During his time at Warner Bros., Avery developed Bugs Bunny, Daffy Duck, and Elmer Fudd into the characters we recognize today. *Blitz Wolf*, Avery's first movie released under the MGM label, begins as a parody of Disney's *Three Little Pigs*. A wartime fable, the short won Avery an Academy Award nomination.

While at Warner Brothers, Tex Avery created one of the most beloved cartoon characters of all time: Bugs Bunny. In the scene above, Bugs utters his famous line, "Ehh . . . what's up, Doc?" to Yosemite Sam in the 1945 short, Hare Trigger, directed by Isadore "Friz" Freleng.

The villain of *Blitz Wolf* is a storm trooper with a German accent who resembles Adolf Hitler. Two of the little pigs build their houses of straw and wood, while Sgt. Pork (a pun on Sgt. York, an actual World War I hero) surrounds his with artillery and trenches.

Making fun of his efforts, the two pigs sing "You'll never get rich by digging a ditch." Sgt. Pork advises his brothers to buy bombs and weapons in preparation for the approaching invasion.

Several times, the characters directly address the audience. The Wolf, for example, challenges the audience to "go on and hiss! Who cares?" Other jokes include a "scream bomb" which forms a mouth and shrieks loudly, an "incendiary bomb" that gives the Wolf a hot foot, and a group of enemy bombs disarmed by viewing a pin-up. The Wolf is finally demolished by Pork's secret weapon, defense bonds.

Despite the anarchy of his cartoons, Avery was a perfectionist when it came to creating them. Animator Michael Lah recalled that when Avery reviewed the pencil tests, he "would want a lot of changes. And, my gosh, even when the animation was on cels, he would cut frames on the Movieola, to get the effect he wanted!"[22]

Although it is the most familiar, hand-drawn cel animation (and now computer animation) is not the only way to animate images. For some types of animation, the animator never even draws a line. Sand, cut or torn paper, models or puppets—just about anything that can be shifted, cut, scattered, or rotated can be animated.

Canadian Norman McLaren made fifty-nine films using many different techniques. He scratched and painted on film stock or made images by removing the emulsion from a film strip. His Oscar-winning 1952 film *Neighbours* used pixilation, a technique that applies stop-motion techniques to filming live actors. In *A Chairy Tale*, a live actor tries to sit in a chair that manages, through animation, to avoid him. *For Pas de deux*, a film of dancers Margeret Mercier and Vincent Warren, McLaren exposed the same frames as many as ten times, creating multiple images of the dancers. McLaren also experimented with creating sound by painting and engraving on film.[23]

> ## PIXILATION—
> Using a technique similar to stop-motion animation, a camera is set to film live action performance at regular intervals. The result is speeded up action that makes the actors seem to float or fly.

American animator Caroline Leaf animated beach sand on a piece of glass in her first film *Sand, or Peter and the Wolf* and in *The Metamorphosis of Mr. Samsa*, based on Franz Kafka's story. For these films, she drew with sand on a glass plate under the camera. Each drawing destroyed the one before it. She used washes of watercolor and ink on paper to capture a family's reactions to a dying grandmother in *The Street*. *Two Sisters* was animated by etching directly on 70mm color film.[24]

Nick Park, a writer, director, producer, and stop-motion animator at Aardman Animation, makes films using plasticine, a putty-like molding material, to create his expressive characters. His characters all feature recognizable, wide "coat-hanger" mouths. *A Grand Day Out*, Park's first film, marked the debut of Wallace, a cheese-obsessed inventor, and his quick-witted dog, Gromit. The two embody typical British character traits. *Creature Comforts* won an Academy Award in 1990. In the five-minute film, man-in-the-street interviews about the state of the world provide dialogue for animals commenting on conditions in their zoo. In 2000, Park and Peter Lord made the full-length clay animation film *Chicken Run*, one of only a few full-length stop-motion features. *Chicken Run*, which took five years to complete, combines stop motion and computer graphics effects.[25]

CLAY ANIMATION—A form of animation in which the figures to be animated are sculpted out of modeling clay and put into motion one frame or movement at a time. Animator Will Vinton dubbed this process *claymation*.

European animation is more influenced by trends in fine art than American animation. Jan Švankmajer, a Czech animator, works in the surrealist tradition. His dark, disturbing films mix clay models, dolls, puppets, masks, carved vegetables, live action film, and stop-motion animation, depending on the medium he thinks will best express his ideas. He has drawn from Edgar Allen

Poe stories, *Alice in Wonderland*, and the Faust legend, but all his films are filled with dreams, fears, and anxieties. For most of his career, Švankmajer worked in Prague under Communist rule, and many of his films have a strong anti-Communist or anti-totalitarian message. Despite limited distribution, his films have influenced several other filmmakers, notably Tim Burton and Terry Gilliam.[26]

COMPUTER GENERATED ANIMATION

CEL ANIMATION MEETS COMPUTER GRAPHICS

Computer generated (CG) animation can look like cel animation as it does in films like *The Incredibles* or, as in *Toy Story*, like stop-motion animation. Using the computer, animators can imitate live action camera moves and angles that would be difficult or impossible to achieve with traditional cel animation: the swoop from the chandelier to the dancing couple in the ballroom scene of *Beauty and the Beast*, for example.

Traditional and CG animation can be combined in other ways. Drawings on cels can be merged with drawings made in a computer.

Or computer-generated visual effects can be blended into live action films, as in *The Lord of the Rings,* so that it is difficult for viewers to tell where reality ends and visual effects begin.

Using a computer, an animator can make any object look exactly like marble or rubber. Once that object is in motion, however, traditional animation concerns take over. A realistic marble object, for example, will move more slowly than a rubber object, because in nature it weighs more.

> **COMPUTER GRAPHICS (CG)** —Any two- or three-dimensional image created entirely within a computer. Also called CGI (computer-generated imagery).

The tools of a traditional animator are paper, pencils, and a registration device—a tool for keeping drawings exactly lined up. The most common registration device is a board with pegs to hold the drawings. A CG animator uses a computer screen, mouse, and keyboard. After images are created in the computer, the digital information is translated into actual frames of film. This is called rendering.[1]

> **REGISTRATION DEVICE**—Any device that keeps an animator's drawings lined up exactly. The most common registration device is a board with pegs to hold the drawings in place.

Studio animation departments now use computers to produce most of their animated films.

RENDER—Translating the information that makes up a movie from digital data into actual frames of film.

Even films and television programs that are mainly hand-drawn may use the computer for animation's tedious work, like producing in-betweens and adding color. Not all animators, however, believe that CG is better than traditional animation methods.

Animator Randy Cartwright sees advantages to traditional animation: "I have complete freedom to draw anything my mind can imagine. I can distort the character to caricature movement, squashing, stretching, making multiple images—anything I think the audience will believe."[2]

CG animators can move the characters using controls or change the size and scale of the parts, but they have limited ability to change a character's shape. "With my pencil, I can physically sculpt this image any way I choose," Cartwright says. "I can see through the paper to compare positioning, and I usually roll the drawings in my fingers to imagine the action."[3]

Czech animator Jan Švankmajer is another who favors traditional animation. He often works with objects he happens to find, and believes that they carry the emotions of the people who have used them. He objects to computer animation "because the objects are created artificially and have no content or soul."[4]

Pixar executive John Lasseter stresses that

computer animation and traditional animation have different strengths:

> I realized that the easiest things to do in hand-drawn animation are the most difficult to do in computer animation. An example of that is organic shapes. . . . That's so hard to do with computer animation; it's virtually impossible. But then trying to animate a room with a moving camera shot in hand animation is also virtually impossible. And also, the shadowing, and shading, and lighting, and reflection, refraction. . . . To me, it's really important for animators to understand the medium they're working in, whether it's sand animation, clay animation, cel animation, or computer animation.[5]

Although it might seem that computer-generated animation is much easier than making thousands of drawings or moving an object bit by bit as in traditional animation, this is not exactly the case. A lot of time-consuming work goes into developing the programs that produce believable, appealing animation.

"Sure, it's all in the computer," Brad Bird, the director of *The Incredibles*, told a reporter. "But you still have to build it, tell the computer how thick something is and assign colors and textures. It's just like you're building a physical set. It takes time."[6]

Each new CG film must solve unique problems, whether it is giving personalities to two desk lamps (*Luxo Jr.*), portraying realistic underwater scenes

(*Finding Nemo*, *Waterworld*), generating a violent tornado (*Twister*), or creating convincing human skin (*The Lord of the Rings*).

TECHNIQUES OF COMPUTER ANIMATION

Unlike traditional animators, computer animators do not draw or paint. When they begin their work, characters, models, layout, dialogue, and the set are already designed and in the computer.

Before the animator begins, a basic model must be constructed. Models are usually made out of traditional materials like clay. Next, a grid is drawn on the surface of the sculpture that divides it into different sized squares. Many small squares cover areas like the face and mouth that use small, subtle movements to talk and show emotion. Less detailed areas and areas that make broad movements are covered with fewer, larger squares.

At this point, the physical model is converted into a computer model. A modeler creates a digital skeleton to fit inside the digital skin, similar to the armature, the underlying framework, of a traditional stop-motion puppet, and adds muscles and flesh. Anything that can be added to a traditional physical model can be added digitally to a digital model, although it is very difficult to create realistic skin and hair.[7]

Once a computer, or virtual,

> ARMATURE—The underlying framework or skeleton of a model or puppet.

model is created, it can be copied over and over to make scenes with hundreds of characters. Visual effects artists working on *The Lord of the Rings* used this ability to help create the vast armies of Orcs and Uruk-hai in those films.

CG animators manipulate their characters like puppeteers. Using controls called avars, or animation variables, which work something like puppet strings, they adjust the character's moveable parts. For example, there will be a control on the character's neck that allows the animator to move its head in several directions.

In *Toy Story*, Mr. Potato Head's mouth needed eight avars to form its basic shape and others to control the mouth's position on the character's face. High level avars control walking,

AVARS—Animated variables that computer animators use to control and change elements of the models.

bending over, and other movements. *Toy Story*'s "Woody" had over 700 avar controls.[8]

After analyzing the scene, the animator decides on the character's performance or actions and sets key poses, similar to extremes in traditional animation. The computer fills in the intermediate drawings or in-betweens.[9]

Because virtual models are not actually solid, CG animators must be careful to check their work from different angles to see how it actually exists in three-dimensional space. Animator Kathy Zielinski emphasizes the importance of this step: "If my character is off balance, or out of registration with his

In Toy Story (1995), the Mr. Potato Head character needed eight avars (which are like animated "puppet strings") to form its basic shape.

props, environment, or other characters, it will not only look strange when he starts to move; it will cause tremendous problems when my co-workers try to light and render the scene later on."[10]

Once the computer records the completed animation, a CG animator can play it back and can see immediately if the animation is working. Changes can be made until the scene is perfected.

The realism of three-dimensional computer-generated animation also means that very exaggerated gestures or lots of squash and stretch may not look as believable as they do in traditional animation. Partly for this reason, director Brad Bird wanted the characters in his film *The Incredibles* to look more like caricatures than like real people.

THE INCREDIBLES

The 2004 animated Pixar film *The Incredibles* broke new ground for a computer-animated movie. For the first time, the Pixar crew created wholly human characters rather than toys or animals. The crew was challenged to come up with new ways of using computers to depict everything from the characters' skin and clothing to lighting, set design, and special effects.

Although the tools are different, animators of the 1940s would find the process used by *The*

Dash, Violet, Mr. Incredible, and Elastigirl (left to right) in a scene from the 2004 movie hit, The Incredibles.

Incredibles filmmakers familiar. In fact, director Brad Bird encouraged his animators to study early animated works. "I was inspired most by the classic Disney animated films like *Lady and the Tramp*, which have such indelible characters that they've stood the test of time. The question was how to do that with the very best tools the art form has to offer today."[11]

The Incredibles concerns a family of superheroes who have been forced to hide their superpowers and live an average, suburban life. Father Bob Parr, also known as Mr. Incredible, has put on weight and works in an insurance office. His wife Helen, the former Elastigirl, has her stretchable hands full taking care of their children. Ten-year-old Dash is barely able to keep his super speed under control. Teenage Violet can make herself invisible. And baby Jack-Jack has not yet discovered his powers. When Bob is lured to a remote island by villainous Syndrome, the Parrs rally to save him.

When they were developing the film's strong, engaging characters and well-structured plot, director Bird and his crew began with a storyboard and animatics, a more technologically advanced version of the pencil test.

ANIMATICS—A film, video, or computer compilation of animators' drawings that allows them to refine sequences before they are actually animated.

ART DEPARTMENT

While the script was being written, the art department

designed every physical detail of the characters, the virtual sets and props, and the color palette. Production designer Lou Romano and art director Ralph Eggleston tweaked the style of 1960s architecture to give Bird the familiar, yet distinctive surroundings he wanted. "I saw the world of *The Incredibles* as looking sort of like what we thought the future would turn out like in the 1960s," Bird explains.[12]

To convey the depressing nature of Bob's life, the designers included shapes that appeared to be pressing down on him, like the angular roof of his house. The rows of cubicles in Bob's office form "X" and "V" shapes and seem to point right at Bob. In contrast, the island's jungle setting has sweeping, nature-inspired lines.[13]

VOICE TRACK

Once the screenplay was completed and the look of the film was set, actors recorded their voice performances. Craig T. Nelson as Bob Parr, Holly Hunter as Helen, Sarah Vowell and Spencer Fox as Violet and Dash, Jason Lee as Syndrome, Samuel L. Jackson as Bob's best friend Lucius Best "Frozone," and Bird himself used their voices to fashion personalities that helped the animators visualize the characters.

ANIMATION

The preliminaries completed, work began on changing two-dimensional storyboard illustrations into film. After the modeling group built characters and sets in the computer, they were fine-tuned by the layout crew. Pixar had never starred human characters in a film because they are the most difficult to animate with a computer. Computers are better at portraying something hard and shiny like the bugs in *A Bug's Life* than something stretchy like skin.

According to Tony Fucile, a supervising animator: "We spend our whole lives watching other humans and we know right away when something, even the smallest little thing, isn't quite right."[14] Bird decided on stylized characters who would hint at reality rather than try to duplicate it. "If you add too many

Several new animation techniques were developed during the creation of The Incredibles. *These techniques helped make the characters' fantastic powers look and flow better than any other animated film before.*

details they end up looking like deformed people," he says.[15]

With the voice track as a guide, they tried to match a character's expressions to the tone of the performance. Animators watched video performances of the actors for clues to realistic facial expressions. As a result, Helen's expressions ended up resembling actress Holly Hunter's.

Brad Bird's characters and story inspired the *Incredibles* team to stretch their technological know-how. Shy, teenage Violet hides her face behind her long hair, so her character needed digital hair that would move and flow in different ways. As Mark Henne, the film's hair and cloth simulation supervisor explains: "Hair in a CG film has always been tough because it's so multi-layered and made up of millions of strands. . . . It breaks apart and re-forms in response to how the head is moving and how the wind is blowing."[16] The assignment proved to be so tough that Violet's hair was one of the last problems the animators solved.

The extreme squash and stretch needed for the character of Elastigirl resulted in the construction of a new computer program called "deformer." Animators also found a way to animate clothes so they mimicked the flutter and swing of actual fabric.

SOUND AND MUSIC

Sound effects and music were added last. In composing music for the film, Michael Giacchino wanted to duplicate the scores of action adventure movies from the 1960s. To do that, he used instruments like xylophones, bongos, and lots of brass. He also created themes, called motifs, for each character. "Basically, the filmmakers told me the story of *The Incredibles*, and I tried to tell it back in musical form," Giacchino says.[17]

It takes many people working in a variety of jobs to make a film as complicated as *The Incredibles*. Some of those different jobs are listed below:[18]

1. *Animation director.* Responsible for overseeing the animation of the project and for hiring the animators. The animation director does the key sketches and supervises voice recordings, timing, and character development.

2. *Animator.* Creates characters' body and facial movements.

3. *Director.* Responsible for overseeing all aspects of the film.

4. *Director of photography.* Responsible, along with the director and production designer, for the final look of the film.

5. *Layout artist.* Realizes set designs based on the storyboards and creates the "camera shots," timing, and movements.

6. *Lighting designer.* Responsible for the different lighting effects on the various sets.

7. *Sculptor.* Translates two-dimensional drawings of a character into a three-dimensional model that

is used during the animation process by sketch artists, computer modelers, and painters.

8. *Set dresser.* Working with the production designer and director, chooses and places all the props, which include vegetation and furnishings.

9. *Set sequence supervisor.* Makes sure that the set designers' artistic vision is effectively realized by the technical crew.

10. *Special effects artist.* Creates special effects such as water, fire, ice, electrical bolts, clouds, and explosions.

11. *Story artist.* Explores the visual possibilities in a scene and tries to uncover any possible dramatic or logistical problems.

12. *Supervising editor.* Together with the director, chooses the most effective shot for each scene, taking into consideration composition, timing, camera angle, and depth of field.

VISUAL EFFECTS:
THEN AND NOW

Visual effects artists make things happen in movies or on television that might not normally occur in real life or "where it's too expensive, too dangerous or impossible" to shoot the real thing, according to visual effects artist John Nelson *(I, Robot).*[1]

Scenes that would be difficult to capture on camera, such as a person diving from a bridge into a raging river, or settings that are too expensive to build like the big city digital backdrops in *The Day After Tomorrow*, are produced by visual effects artists. When more snow is needed in a winter scene, or telephone wires show up in a historical movie, visual effects artists correct the shots. Computers can create digital tears or blood, embellish backgrounds and sets, make a small crowd seem large, or touch up actors' wrinkles and flaws.

Like animators, visual effects artists take a drawing, a model, or other inanimate object and, using animation techniques, make it seem real. Lasers, lightening bolts, and other similar features are drawn by hand, animated, and added to live action films.[2] Rotoscoping, the animation technique developed by Max Fleischer in the 1930s, was used to create shadows of space ships and to produce other visual effects in the 1977 film *Star Wars*. The 1993 film *Jurassic Park* combined stop-motion animation with computer-generated images to bring the dinosaurs to life.

Visual effects artists often work together with makeup artists, costume designers, cinematographers, and stunt actors to create modern movie effects. Makeup, costumes, color, and lighting can all be perfected in the computer, and physical effects such as explosions and stunts can be enhanced. A star's face can be inserted on the body of a stunt performer, or the computer can combine live actors with animated actors as in *Stuart Little*.

Just because visual effects can re-create almost any image the director would like does not

MINIATURE—Any object or location that is reproduced at a smaller than life-size scale for filming purposes.

In 1993, audiences were stunned by how real the dinosaur's appeared on the screen in Jurassic Park.

mean that visual effects are always the best choice. Although digital doubles were used for some of the actors in *Spider-Man 2*, visual effects supervisor Scott Stodyk advises: "There's so much subtlety and creativity that an actor brings to the table. It's hard to replace that with an animator."[3]

> MODEL—Any object or location that has been reproduced for filming purposes.

KING KONG (1933): SETTING THE STANDARD

Willis O'Brien, visual effects designer for *King Kong*, began his career doing stop-motion animation. O'Brien used many different techniques, including stop-motion animation, miniatures, models, rear projection, miniature rear projection, traveling mattes, matte painting, and optical effects to create the lost prehistoric world where the giant ape King Kong is discovered.

Techniques developed by O'Brien, Marcel Delgado, Linwood Dunn, and others for *King Kong* are still used by visual effects artists today, although they now may be created in the computer.

Sets

Rather than travel to Africa for expensive location shooting, the filmmakers created Skull Island, the jungle setting of the lost world, in the studio. O'Brien built small sets that resembled French artist Gustave

Doré's engravings for the book *Paradise Lost* by John Milton. His first sets used small living plants, which had to be replaced because their growth, although invisible to the eye, was obvious when the stop-motion footage was projected at a normal speed.[4]

> **REAR PROJECTION—** A method of combining live-action foregrounds with pre-filmed background scenery.

After that experiment, miniature jungle sets were decorated with trees made from branches covered with toilet paper and modeling clay. Sheet metal was used for palm fronds. Vine roots and dried moss filled out the background. O'Brien even made tiny birds fly through the landscape using piano wire to support them.[5]

> **MINIATURE REAR PROJECTION—**Projection of filmed live action onto small screens erected in miniature sets.

Settings were created using a combination of miniatures and matte paintings on glass. In some of the jungle scenes, O'Brien used as many as three planes of painted glass to create foreground, middle distance, and background, with miniature set elements inserted between them.[6] When the planes were lined up and lighted, the jungle scenes looked realistically deep.

Models

Skull Island is inhabited by Kong, a fifty-foot ape, as well as dinosaurs and a giant snake. Animators studied Eadweard Muybridge's photographs of animals in motion and slow-motion films of elephants for ideas of how these large creatures might move.[7]

Miniature animated models were used to portray the creatures. To assemble the models, Marcel Delgado used a build-up technique he had developed while working with O'Brien on the 1925 film *The Lost World*.

First, he created an anatomically correct steel armature or skeleton with jointed spine and tiny ball-and-socket joints for every moving limb. To re-create delicate movements of lips, eyebrows, and other facial muscles, wire inserts were added to the skeletons. Some models, for example the stegosaurus, were fitted with air bladders that could be inflated and deflated to mimic breathing.

> MATTE—Something used to mask off a selected area of the camera's field of view. Aids double exposures by blocking off the section of the picture that does not change.

> TRAVELING MATTE—Traveling mattes are used to combine two separately filmed elements when the foreground element (a person, for example) changes shape or position from frame to frame, necessitating a new matte for each frame. Today, most traveling mattes are created digitally.

After the models were padded with cotton and pieces of sponge molded to represent muscle and flesh, Delgado gave them a liquid latex skin. Surface textures, such as scales, were cast in latex and placed on the skin one by one before the model was painted.[8]

Models were also made of the lead actors. A model of actress Fay Wray, who plays Ann Darrow, was used when Kong carries Ann through the jungle after he captures her. Models of Wray and actor Bruce Cabot were used to show them dangling at the end of a rope when their characters try to escape from Kong.[9]

Kong, the giant ape, was the visual effects masterpiece of the film. Although crude by today's standards, nothing as realistic had been seen before in movies. The character was portrayed in most scenes by an eighteen-inch puppet covered in bear fur. Delgado stretched rubber tendons between Kong's joints for a realistic, sinewy appearance.

For close-ups, a giant head, an arm, a hand, and a foot of Kong were constructed. The giant models used a wood and metal frame interwoven with cloth and covered, like the miniatures, with bearskins. The giant head had a two-foot nose and four-foot eyebrows and its plaster eyes were twelve inches in diameter. Three to four men inside Kong's head operated the cables, levers, and compressed-air devices that controlled his features.[10]

OPTICAL EFFECTS—
All effects that are not done physically but are made using cameras, computers, and other technology.

MATTE PAINTING—A large painting used to depict backgrounds too costly to create or find. Matte paintings can be painted directly within a computer.

70

Traveling Mattes

Linwood G. Dunn was in charge of the optical effects for the film. To portray Kong's first appearance in the native village, Dunn used a process called a traveling matte or blue screen.[11]

A matte is like a mask and is used to prevent a portion of film from being exposed. A stationary

King Kong beats back a pterodactyl with his right hand while holding actress Fay Wray in his left in King Kong *(1933).*

matte covers a fixed area. A traveling matte follows the silhouette of a moving character or object and is different for each frame of the film. Today, similar effects are created using digital compositing and a green screen process.

> ## BLUE SCREEN PROCESS—
> An optical process by which subjects filmed in front of a blue screen are combined with a separately filmed background. Digital processes can produce a matte from a surface painted blue, green, or any other consistent color.

Rear Projection

Rear projection is used to put real-life actors in the same scene with animated creatures. In rear projection, the camera shoots actors performing in front of a translucent screen while a previously filmed scene is projected on the back of the screen. In *King Kong*, one such scene shows Fay Wray trapped in a tree in the live foreground while Kong battles with a dinosaur in the projected background.[12]

Miniature rear projection, developed for *King Kong*, projects previously filmed live action footage into a miniature setting. Small screens made of stretched sheets of surgical rubber were inserted into the miniature jungle. Images of the actors were then rear-projected onto these screens one frame at a time, so they would match the creature animation.[13]

> ## COMPOSITING—
> A method of blending separate visual components into one shot.

Miniature rear projection was used in many

scenes, including one when the character John Driscoll, played by Bruce Cabot, hides from Kong in a cave. A miniature cliff was built with a small cave in its wall and a rear-projection screen just inside the cave. Live action film of Cabot performing in a large-scale cave set was projected on the screen one frame at a time. A model of Kong was animated on the cliff above. The shot was later edited together with a close-up of Cabot fighting off a giant mechanical ape arm that reached into the cave.[14]

For the New York scenes, miniatures of the Empire State Building and many other landmarks were built. The four Navy pursuit planes shown attacking Kong when he climbs the Empire State Building were real planes in some of the scenes. Miniature planes built to four different scales were also used in scenes where they were flying in close-up near Kong.[15]

Each special effects scene was worked out first in detailed drawings and in three-dimensional models. All the effort paid off for the filmmakers and for RKO Radio Pictures, which produced the film. *King Kong* was so successful that its profits saved the studio from bankruptcy.[16]

THE LORD OF THE RINGS: RAISING THE BAR

Today, the visual effects in *King Kong*, although beautiful, look somewhat fake and stagy. Contemporary audiences are used to the realistic visual effects that computer graphics produce for films like *Pleasantville* and *The Matrix*. The three films that make up *The Lord of the Rings* series used cutting-edge computer technology to build landscapes and characters and create a realistic, but imaginary, universe.

The Lord of the Rings books by J.R.R. Tolkien are filled with descriptions of spectacular landscapes, castles and fortresses, armor and weaponry, dwarfs, elves, diminutive Hobbits, giants, wizards, and other fantasy creatures, imaginary animals, twisting caverns, and fiery volcanoes.

When director Peter Jackson began work on the films based on the books, he planned to bring all this to the screen in a believable way. The ground-breaking visual effects in the three films were designed and built by Weta Digital, a visual effects facility in Wellington, New Zealand.

Initial designs and storyboards were based on illustrations drawn for the books by Alan Lee and John Howe. Because he loved their illustrations, Jackson hired the two men to design the films: "Alan Lee's artwork has a beauty and lyricism about it. His art captured what I hoped to capture with the film, which is a sort of graceful and gentle feeling. . . . John Howe is a master of capturing exciting moments. His artwork is almost like looking at a freeze-frame from the movie."[17]

The members of the Fellowship of the Ring—an elf, a dwarf, and four Hobbits, as well as several men and a wizard—travel across all of Middle-Earth and encounter a range of landscapes. More than sixty-five different miniature sets were used, including various cities, forests, Helm's Deep, volcanoes, and caves.[18] Computers were used to blend miniatures and digital shots with footage shot on location in the New Zealand landscape.

In the first film of the trilogy, the wizard Gandalf is seen approaching the fortress of Isengard, home of corrupt wizard Saruman. Except for shots of Gandalf on horseback, everything in the scene was created in the computer. The background is a composite of the base of a mountain, a valley, several other mountain ranges, and a miniature of the Isengard tower.

Alan Lee's sketches of Orthanc, the Isengard tower, were used as blueprints for the miniatures crew. The tower, which looks as if it were made from the glassy black volcanic stone obsidian, was cast in wax and then carved to give it a splintered appearance.[19]

Although called a miniature, the Isengard set was not small. The tower, built at a 1/35th scale, stood nearly fifteen feet high. And the Isengard plain stretched over sixty-five feet. According to miniature builder John Baster: "[Weta effects supervisor] Richard Taylor really likes to make the biggest, most detailed models that you can possibly build. That's where a lot of the realism is achieved."[20] The visual effects crew was responsible not only for creating all the different settings that Tolkien described in the books, but also many imaginary characters such as Ents, the tree-like guardians of the forest, and enormous armies of Orcs and Uruk-hai. Architecture, costume, armor, and props were used to give each society and culture its own look.

The Hobbits

The Hobbits, a small, round people with hairy feet, were played by normal-sized actors Elijah Wood, Billy Boyd, Sean Astin, and Dominic Monaghan. The actors were fitted with hairy prosthetic, or artificial, feet and pointy ears.

Various techniques were then used to make them seem smaller than regular humans. In some scenes, the actors playing Hobbits kneeled, while the full-sized humans stood on a small crate. Scenes that showed different-sized characters moving in the same set were filmed twice, using a computer-controlled camera. Richard Taylor explains: "The actors playing the large-sized people were filmed first; then the camera's movements were repro-grammed to film a second run-through with the frame a third larger and the movements magnified likewise. When the two frames were digitally combined, the Hobbit appeared relatively smaller than the other actors."[21]

> **PROSTHETICS—**
> False limbs, noses, or other appendages that are attached to the face or body of a performer.

The Ents

Many others creatures were completely animated in the computer and seamlessly integrated with the live actors. The Ents were mainly computer animated. To animate Treebeard, the oldest Ent, a fifteen-foot tall animatronic was built, based on sketches by Alan Lee and Grant Major. An animatronic is a remote-controlled system using various mechanical devices to produce a life-like perform-ance in models or puppets. The animatronic Treebeard was used in scenes where the Ent had to perform with live actors. Using this model as a guide, a digital version was created, which allowed the animators to perfect the character's more delicate movements and expressions in the computer.[22]

> **ANIMATRONIC—** A remote-controlled system that uses mechanical devices to produce a life-like performance using puppets or models.

Orcs and Uruk-hai

Fierce battles take up much of *The Lord of the Rings* trilogy. To create the masses of evil Orcs and Uruk-hai warriors, the filmmakers used a combination of special effects makeup and computer-generated images.

Stunt actors wearing full special effects makeup, including artificial eyebrows, noses and chins, contact lenses, wigs, and false teeth performed closest to the cameras. Extras wearing less realistic latex and foam rubber masks were placed behind them. And thousands of three-dimensional computer-generated Orcs and Uruk-hai were added to the background of the battle scenes during post-production.[23]

Creating the computer-generated creatures involved several steps. Dozens of models of the warriors were scanned into the computer and given three-dimensional articulated skeletons, muscles, and other details. Once the CG warriors were built, they had to be animated on the battlefield. Taylor explains how that was accomplished:

> Since it was impossible to animate them one by one, we got the idea to give each of them an artificial intelligence and a "vocabulary" of warrior poses. Using the Massive program (developed by Weta Graphics), thousands of characters advance in the direction we chose, acting in a realistic manner and reacting to the presence of the other characters around them like individuals with free will.[24]

Gollum

The most revolutionary visual effect in *The Lord of the Rings* is the character Gollum, a skinny being, who is physically and mentally corrupted by the all-powerful ring. Having decided that Gollum would be impossible to duplicate using makeup and prosthetics, Peter Jackson chose to create the character digitally.

Actor Andy Serkis acts out the part of Gollum (from The Lord of the Rings *trilogy) in his motion-capture costume.*

As the animators of *Snow White* and *The Incredibles* knew, the more "realistic" a human character looks in animation, the less believable it is. Brad Bird handled the problem by purposely making his characters look more cartoonish. Gollum's creators went in the other direction and brought all of their technical expertise to making the character look convincingly human.

MOTION CAPTURE— Also called performance capture. A method of capturing the natural movement of bodies or faces so that it can be used for animating computer-generated characters.

A process called motion capture was the basis for Gollum's animation. Motion capture uses live action performances as a pattern for animated characters. Actor Andy Serkis performed in the studio wearing a white, blue, or green costume, which would be digitally erased during editing. Markers attached to his feet, shins, knees, hips, elbows, shoulders, wrists, hands, and his head were recorded by twenty-five special electronic cameras, making a digital record of the actor's every move.

SUBSURFACE SCATTERING— describes what happens when light strikes a translucent surface, spreads inside the material, and then is either absorbed or leaves the surface from a different point.

CG animators used a process similar to rotoscoping to reproduce Gollum's features on the actor's body. The creature's facial expressions were hand-animated.[25]

Human skin, with its pores, wrinkles, hair, and scars is particularly difficult to replicate in the computer. Skin also reflects light differently than solid objects do. To make realistic skin for Gollum, the technicians used a number of different techniques to scatter light and add texture, surface details, and shadows. Subsurface scattering—a new approach to character lighting that duplicates the effect of light striking a translucent surface—was used for the first time in this film.[26]

5

ANIMATION AND VISUAL EFFECTS ON TELEVISION

When economics drove cartoons and short animated films out of movie theaters, they found a home on television. Animated series such as Jay Ward's *The Rocky and Bullwinkle Show* and Hanna-Barbera's *The Flintstones* were popular during the 1960s. But television typically has smaller budgets than movies, so animators had to find ways to produce a less expensive product.

Limited cel animation was one way that costs could be held down. Limited cel animation reduces the number of drawings that appear in a minute's worth of film by making new drawings only for the part of a scene that changes. For example, when a character is talking, only its mouth will move while the rest of the character is illustrated by the same drawing throughout.

Limited cel animation does not have the detail and realism of theatrical animation. However, because it is not bound by the requirements of realism, animators are more likely to experiment with different artistic styles. Television animation is not as visually compelling as full cel animated films, making television programs more dependent on sophisticated writing, verbal humor, and voice talent.[1]

> **LIMITED CEL ANIMATION—** Animation drawn on the smallest number of cels possible.

To animate repetitive motion like walking, cycles (an animation process similar to a tape loop) are used to save the animator's time. For example, in animating a walk, the artist will plan out a sequence so that the last drawing leads back into the first drawing. Only the character's legs move, while the body stays in the same position. The same drawings can then be repeated until the character has walked for the necessary amount of time.[2] This process is easily repeated to fit other, similar character activities.

> **CYCLES—**A method of animating in which an action such as walking takes place in a continuous loop.

Cels and sequences of cels are re-used in limited animation to further cut animation costs. Once the animator has drawn a character driving a car, for example, the same sequence is used every time the character needs to drive a car.

CREATING A CARTOON SERIES:
THE SIMPSONS

By 1987, when cartoonist Matt Groening was asked by the producers of *The Tracey Ullman Show* to make a few very short animated films to appear between live action sketches on the program, cartoons in the United States were generally thought of as something only children would watch.

The first episode of *The Simpsons* was broadcast on the April 19, 1987 episode of *The Tracey Ullman Show* and lasted fourteen seconds.[3] Drawing and animation were crude and two-dimensional and used bright, primary colors. Over two years later, the popularity of the wickedly funny cartoon convinced the Fox Network to make *The Simpsons* into a separate series. The first full-length episode, a parody of typical Christmas stories such as *A Christmas Carol* and *Miracle on 34th Street*, premiered in December 1989.

Springfield, the town where the Simpsons live, resembles towns in American television comedies from the 1950s through the 1970s. It is, however, full of strange, unlikely characters. The show focuses on the day-to-day troubles of a family with a stay-at-home mother, a father who works at a nuclear power plant, and three children. Their names—Homer, Marge, Lisa, and Maggie—were adopted from Groening's own family. The name "Bart," however, came from scrambling the letters of the word "brat," which appropriately described the character's personality.

Families had been featured before in television animated series such as *The Flintstones* and *The Jetsons*, but those characters were not quite as easy to identify with as the Simpson family. The series was intended to poke fun at popular, more sentimental, family comedies such as *The Cosby Show,* which were popular when *The Simpsons* began.

Groening had more on his mind than poking fun at the American family. "It always amazes me how few cartoonists in print or animation go after the bigger issues, the kinds of things that keep you lying awake in the middle of the night—questions about death and love and sex and work and relationships. And that's what I'm trying to do," he explains.[4]

The Simpsons, which uses limited cel animation, is distinguished by its concept and writing. Although at least one gag paid tribute to Chuck Jones's gravity-defying Wile E. Coyote, Groening's characters usually act and move like real people. As a rule, there are no talking animals or objects; however, more fantastic elements are brought into the mix during dream sequences.

Like *The Rocky and Bullwinkle Show*, *The Simpsons* often parodies popular culture. Halloween episodes have spoofed *King Kong*, *Dracula*, and zombie movies. *The Itchy & Scratchy Show*, a cartoon series watched by Bart and Lisa, satirizes

Animator and director Chuck Jones at work drawing a cel of Bugs Bunny some time circa 1960. Although originally produced for theatre viewing, Bugs Bunny cartoons became a staple of Saturday morning television.

classic cartoons like *Tom & Jerry*. Some episodes have considered controversial topics including mass media, religion, medical issues, consumerism, and politics. The show appeals to sophisticated and unsophisticated viewers on different levels.

As Groening intended, the program also has a strong emotional base. The Simpsons may be a dysfunctional family, but they are loyal to each other.

Over time, the characters have become more complex, and their personalities have developed.

The first animators, David Silverman and Wes Archer, chose the color palette and other key details to embellish Groening's rough black-and-white sketches. They decided on a limited palette of 200 colors as opposed to the approximately 1,000–2,000 colors used in a typical animated feature or CG cartoon.[5]

Gabor Csupo, a head of the animation studio that produced the first few seasons of the show, said:

> We wanted to make shocking colors, like the bright yellow faces and the blue hair on Marge. When they saw it, [the network] screamed; they didn't wanna do it. And we said, "Why? These are the craziest characters, why do you want normal color?"[6]

At first, the animators tried to preserve the sharp angles and crudely-drawn style of the Tracey Ullman episodes. They discovered, as Disney animators had, that to draw characters quickly and in quantity their outlines had to be slightly rounded.[7]

It can take as long as eight to ten months from the first draft of the script to produce the finished half-hour show. (Like all half-hour television series, the actual show lasts only about 20 minutes. The rest of the time is filled by commercials.) That includes two to three months for writing the story and six to seven months for recording, sound mixing, animating, and editing. Because it takes so long to complete each show, several episodes are always in progress at the same time.

The Script

Every episode of the show begins with a script. Before the script is written, a writer "pitches" or presents his idea to the rest of the team. The team then works together to develop the idea until they have outlined a story. The script may be rewritten six to eight times before it is given to voiceover actors for rehearsal.

After the actors read the script aloud for an audience of writers, producers, and others, including Matt Groening, it is rewritten again, perhaps several times. Changes may be made because lines do not sound funny when read aloud or to include new ideas or scenes that enhance the story. Sometimes the rewritten or polished script will include ad libs made by the actors during the recording session.[8]

The writers work under an executive producer known as the show runner. This person (or team) is responsible for all aspects of the production. The show runner makes sure the script is as good as possible, supervises the animation director, makes sure the animation and the writing complement each other, and works with the voice actors and the composer.[9]

The Voice Track

When the script has been polished, the voice actors, including Nancy Cartwright, Hank Azaria, Dan

Castellaneta, Yeardley Smith, and Harry Shearer, meet again to make the actual recording that will be used on the show. Actors usually do several different readings of each scene, so that the editor has a choice of takes. Once the voice track is recorded, the editor and show runner combine the best takes until they have about twelve to fifteen minutes of sequential dialogue.[10] The completed recording is then ready for animation.

Animation

Storyboard artists design the overall look for each particular episode. The animation director then takes charge. He or she must understand filmmaking, camera angles, lighting, wardrobe, and timing. If the episode is supposed to parody a film like *King Kong* or *Citizen Kane*, the animation director must figure out how to suggest the look of that film without directly copying it. Working from the voice tape, the animation director figures out the timing of each scene.

Designers

After the storyboard is approved, the character designer creates any new characters needed for the episode. These are checked by Groening to make sure they fit the style he created. Other designers ensure that backgrounds agree with the standard created for the show and that props visually enhance the jokes and the characters.

Layout

Layout artists create the key poses for each scene, using the storyboard as a guide. The voice track gives the artist clues to the strength of a feeling or the mood of the scene. Once the layout is approved, an animator adds frames that expand and connect the key drawings. A black and white video animatic is used to set the timing of each scene. and to determine if additional changes need to be made.

Timing

The sheet timer writes down how many frames it takes for a character to get from one position to another and how long the camera should hold each moment. Every movement, including walking, blinking, or waving a hand, is recorded. There is even a person who determines how many times a character's mouth should change shape when he or she delivers a line of dialogue.

Color

The color department assigns one of the series' 200 colors to each item. Because it takes around 20,000 to 33,000 drawings for one show,[11] the key artwork cels, detailed timing sheets, and color assignments used to be sent to Korea to be copied and hand-painted. Now computer digital ink and paint technology is used.[12] Until recently, *The Simpsons* was hand drawn but is now completely computer animated.[13]

Music and Sound

Finally, the music, including original songs and sound effects, are added. To create the sound of Bart's heart being ripped out of his chest, for example, the sound effects artist recorded himself punching his fist inside a watermelon and squishing it around.[14]

Groening specified that *The Simpsons* should always be scored with acoustic music, so every episode is accompanied by a 35-piece orchestra.[15] A number of episodes have featured songs written specifically for the show. Like the stories, the lyrics and music of the songs often parody various pop songs.

The Simpsons is the longest running prime time cartoon in American television history. It won a Peabody Award for "providing exceptional animation and stinging social satire, both commodities which are in extremely short supply in television today"[16] and has won numerous Emmy Awards. "Part of the reason that we are still around is that there is a real emotional depth to these characters," creator Matt Groening says.[17]

VISUAL EFFECTS ON THE SMALL SCREEN

Visual effects are a part of many television programs, commercials, and music videos. Viewers expect fantasy shows like *Buffy the Vampire Slayer, Star Trek*, or similar programs to use them.

ANIME AND MANGA

Anime, or Japanese animation, is popular in Japan with both adults and children. Anime has as many genres, or types, as live action cinema. Among them are adventure, science fiction, children's stories, romance, medieval fantasy, erotica, occult/horror, and action. Anime style is influenced by Japanese comic books, called manga, which are closer to graphic novels than American comic books. Some anime are based on popular manga, and manga will sometimes draw their characters and stories from anime. The range of manga and anime make them as popular with adults as they are with children.

Anime has a different style than American and European animation. To save money, limited animation is widely used, resulting in jerky movements and a dependence on extreme close-ups that fill the screen. Some anime artists like Hideo Miyazaki (*Howl's Moving Castle*), draw backgrounds by hand rather than in the computer, resulting in more interesting textures and a three-dimensional appearance.

Large, saucer-like eyes are a distinctive feature of anime. Their use is attributed to Osamu Tezuka, a pioneer of early anime. Inspired by the exaggerated features of Western cartoon characters like Betty Boop and Mickey Mouse, Tezuka believed that large eyes were better at expressing emotions and ideas.

One of the first films featuring Manga-style animation (or anime) that found a larger audience outside of Japan was Akira *(1988).*

The Discovery Channel's *When Dinosaurs Roamed America* is an example of another show that uses visual effects. However, viewers may not be aware that other programs depend on effects to save money and time. About forty percent of visual effects work is done for television.[18]

The television series *ER* is set in Chicago but is usually filmed in Los Angeles. The Chicago skyline, its elevated train, and even snowy Chicago weather are created digitally and added to footage of the actors and sets. Visual effects like these are popular with television producers because they save money. "It could cost *ER* $150,000 to send a crew and cast to Chicago," said Sam Nicholson, chief executive of Stargate Digital, the company that creates *ER*'s effects.[19]

Visual effects also save time, an important factor for a weekly television program. A half-hour television program is usually shot over the course of about five days, and on the average it takes only eight days to shoot an hour-long program. In contrast, a two-hour movie can take from six months to a year to complete. "We can change the sky in twenty minutes on the computer rather than waiting for two days for the weather to break," Nicholson points out.[20]

CBS's crime series, *CSI: Crime Scene Investigation*, *CSI: Miami,* and *CSI: New York*, use visual effects to show various states of decomposition in corpses and to visualize the damage fatal injuries do to the body. In ABC's *Alias*, secret agent

Among the many pioneering special effects used on the 1960s series Star Trek *was when members of the* Enterprise *would "beam down" to a planet's surface from aboard the starship.*

Sydney Bristow, played by Jennifer Garner, travels to locations around the world. In real life Garner acts in front of a green screen, and effects supervisor Kevin Blank plugs in stock footage of each program's setting.[21]

Animators and visual effects artists from Tex Avery to Faith and John Hubley to Will Vinton have made television commercials. Stop-motion animator Vinton used claymation to animate dancing raisins in a series of commercials he made for the California Raisin Board.

More television commercials than not include some form of animation or visual effects. Commercials for M&Ms combine large, animated candies with live actors. Visual effects are used to show cars and other vehicles climbing isolated plateaus or crossing difficult terrain.

Commercials usually have relatively high budgets. Independent animators often fund their own films by making commercials and music videos. Bill Plympton (*Guard Dog*) animated a Peter Himmelman song for the music video *245 Days* and also produced a number of MTV station identifications in between making his own shorts and features.[22]

Music videos also use visual effects to sell their product. The video for Missy Elliot's "Pass that Dutch" used blue screen, rotoscoping, and compositing to show her dropping into a dance sequence while a spaceship hovers over a skyscraper.[23]

Michael Jackson's four-million-dollar music video "Black or White" used morphing, a computer graphics process that had been used in *Terminator 2: Judgment Day*. Morphing, which makes one image appear to transform seamlessly into another, is used in the video to metamorphose fifteen different people. A pale woman with red hair merges into a man with dreadlocks, who becomes an Indian woman, and so on.[24]

Few music videos have this kind of budget, however. Elad Offer, whose video for Outkast's "Hey Ya" earned an MTV award for visual effects, states: "The unfortunate situation is that budgets have dropped considerably . . . so we had to divert some of our attention to commercials."[25]

Several prominent visual effects artists got their start in television. Karen Goulekas, who created visuals of a major storm smashing into New York City for *Day After Tomorrow*, began her career doing effects for television commercials. "[There] you have to do it all," she says, "model, light, animate and composite."[26] Erik Nash spent seven years doing motion-control photography for *Star Trek: The Next Generation* before he moved on to *Apollo 13* and *Titanic*. Jim Rygiel (*The Lord of the Rings*) produced a CG Sony Walkman commercial, among others, before moving into film. John Monos, lead lighting artist on *Spider-Man* and *Spider-Man 2*, learned the ropes "making cereal boxes dance" in television commercials.[27]

VISUAL EFFECTS IN THEME PARKS

Visual effects are not used only in movies and on television. Theme parks such as Universal Studio Tours, Disneyland, Legoland, Tokyo Disney, and others use many different types of visual effects and animation.

In 1965, animator Bill Justice (*Bambi*, *Fantasia*, *Alice in Wonderland*) helped upgrade the attractions at Disneyland. He programmed audio-animatronics figures for "Pirates of the Caribbean," "Haunted Mansion," and others. These life-sized figures controlled by internal mechanisms included synchronized sound so that they appeared to be speaking. Animator Marc Davis (*Sleeping Beauty*) helped develop the sixty-four humans and fifty-five animals included in "Pirates of the Caribbean."[28]

> **AUDIO-ANIMATRONICS—**
> Animatronics with synchronized voice tracks.

When the Experience Music Project (EMP) in Seattle opened, part of the "Funk Blast" ride featured a film of singer James Brown. The film merged an animation of Brown's face as he appeared in 1971 onto the head of Tony Wilson, a young dancer, who mimicked Brown's dancing style during live-action photography.[29]

"StormRider" at Tokyo DisneySea takes the audience on a simulated flight through the eye of a powerful storm. Seats in the passenger compartment are mounted on machinery that pitches and rolls. High resolution film is projected on a curved screen designed to look as if it is being viewed from cockpit windows. The storm, clouds, and various kinds of water were created digitally.[30]

Universal City Studios Tour's "The Revenge of the Mummy" blends a rollercoaster ride with huge CGI mummies that appear to be inches away from the riders.[31] For "Shrek 4-D," film and special effects are combined to let the audience feel, as well as hear and see, the action.[32]

CAREERS IN ANIMATION AND VISUAL EFFECTS

Animators have backgrounds in many different fields, including painting, sculpting, cartooning, model-making, and photography. Computer animators and visual effects artists add to this biology, physics, mathematics, and other sciences. What they all have in common, however, is a love of the medium.

Many, like Bill Plympton, whose 1987 short *Your Face* was nominated for an Oscar, knew they wanted to make films from an early age. "I was first aware of animation at around the age of four or five, when I first saw Daffy Duck . . . that's when I decided to be an animator."[1]

Pixar executive John Lasseter discovered

his future profession at the movies: "I can tell you *exactly* when I realized that I wanted to be an animator. It was at a screening of *The Sword and the Stone* at the local theater. . . . It was the Wardman Theater in Whittier. . . . My mom picked me up, and I said, 'I want to work for Disney. I want to be an animator.'"[2]

Others started out intending to do something completely different. Visual effects supervisor Peter Travers received a B.S. in mechanical engineering from the Worcester Polytechnic Institute.

> My plan was to become a mechanical engineer and analyze the stress on pipe bearings for thirty years. I could draw when I was a kid, [but] I never thought I'd be able to apply that. Then the computer-generated stuff started to come with *Jurassic Park* and whatnot. I did more research on it and decided it was something I could do.[3]

Matt Groening, the creator of *The Simpsons*, began drawing cartoons when he was a student at Evergreen State College in Olympia, Washington, but didn't see it as a career: "My goal in life was to be a writer. . . . [I] did cartooning as this other thing and [never] expected it to be part of how [I] paid the rent."[4]

EDUCATION

As in all artistic fields, education is not a prerequisite for finding work. Schools can teach techniques and develop talents. They can also be a source of

101

contacts in the industry. However, many people working in animation and visual effects got their jobs by asking questions, meeting people, and constantly perfecting their craft. Some companies—Pixar is one—are less interested in where potential employees went to school than in the work they present in their portfolios or videotape reels.

Before becoming an animator, Chuck Jones studied art at Chouinard in Los Angeles. He recommends an art background for all animators: "We can teach an artist to animate; we cannot take the time or expend the effort to teach him to be an artist."[5]

In the 1970s, John Lasseter attended the Disney Character Animation program run by the California Institute of the Arts, established by Walt and Roy Disney in 1961. "When I was graduating from high school, Cal Arts was forming their character animation program as a separate program from the film graphics program. . . . I went there for four years, then went to work for Disney."[6]

Other animators learn their craft through practical experience. Stop-motion animator Nick Park reflects on his lack of formal training:

> When looking back on my education, it is interesting to note that I was largely self taught and didn't actually have any formal animation training! The courses I attended were unstructured and although I enjoyed this freedom, I sometimes missed a more formal approach. . . .

ANIMATOR SALARIES

Starting Salary	Experienced Salary	Star Salary
As low as $30,000	Up to $100,000–175,000	Millions (?)

The average salary for an animator in the United States is about $55,000, but if you are working freelance or on your own projects, rather than for an employer, your annual income can be much lower. With some experience under your belt, and a job at one of the large animation studios, you can expect to earn anywhere from $50,000 to $100,000 a year. As the computer animation industry continues to expand, demand for animators will probably drive salaries higher.

VISUAL EFFECTS SALARIES

Starting Salary	Experienced Salary	Star Salary
As low as $20,000	Up to $150,000–170,000	Millions (?)

Many visual effects artists start off on tasks such as making color corrections or removing flaws from individual frames of film. These jobs generally have long hours and low pay. Although the visual effects field is expanding, employers often take on staff to work only for the duration of a particular project. Like many people in the entertainment industry, visual effects artists are independent agents rather than staff employees. The most successful are sought out for major projects and can earn $200,000 or more a year. Others may work sporadically, making good money one year, but little or nothing another year.

Overall the most valuable aspect of my education has been to make my own films without commercial pressure and to nurture my own style and ideas.[7]

ADVICE

Stephen Schaffer, supervising editor on *The Incredibles*, gives this advice to aspiring editors: "Go to Hollywood and don't be afraid to do anything. I was a production assistant and on my off hours at 8:00 P.M. I would sit for hours and watch the editor."[8]

Visual effects artist, Jim Rygiel (*The Lord of the Rings*) completed a degree in architecture at the University of Wisconsin-Milwaukee and later studied art at Otis Art Institute in Los Angeles. Breaking into the business involved "a lot of networking, knocking on the doors every couple of months. . . . I kept getting turned away but it got me to know the people there [in the industry]."[9]

Visual effects supervisor Ellen Poon (*Men in Black*) studied mathematics at the University of London. She now works for Industrial Light and Magic. She advises students interested in computer animation to "look into doing biology to help you understand animal anatomy. And also, mathematics, and then maybe drawing and painting . . . and design, because design ties everything in together. And you want to get into the computer science part . . ."[10]

John Dykstra was twenty-seven when he invented motion-control photography while working on *Star Wars*. Although he works constantly with advanced technology, he warns against thinking that technology is enough: "It isn't, 'can you make it look real?' It's having done it, is it evocative of an emotion?" He adds, "You have to get life experiences. . . . Exposing yourself to reality is critical to making the virtual real."[11]

Nick Park at work with his famous creations, Wallace and Gromit, in his animation studio in Bristol, England.

Lyndon Barrois agrees with Dykstra's advice: "Contrary to general belief, you don't have to take computer science classes to learn to animate with a computer. What you DO have to learn is how to animate, how to apply the fundamentals to the machine."[12]

Finally, some well-meaning advice to ignore, as Nick Park did: "By the age of twelve years, my fervor for drawing had not abated; school notebooks were covered in cartoons. This brought me to the attention

VIDEO ON THE WEB

The World Wide Web has proven to be an excellent outlet for filmmakers who are just starting out. Sites such as YouTube, Google video, Yahoo! video, and iFilm allow their users to put their original videos on display for the whole world to see. These and other websites have spawned the phenomenon of "viral video"—which is what happens when a video file is emailed/ shared with friends, who in turn forward the video to their other friends, who forward it to still other friends, and so on. This is a quick and easy way to reach the public with your film, but getting your work noticed could be difficult. YouTube, for example, had 9 million unique visitors to its site in February 2006, and was showing more than 40 million videos a day at that time.[14]

of one teacher who said, 'Park, you will never make a living out of cartoons, it's just not art!'"[13]

Many schools offer courses in animation or computer graphics. Some, like the California Institute of the Arts, have made this field a specialty, but as is apparent from the comments above, many different kinds of study can help prepare future animators and visual effects artists. The most important preparation is to learn and perfect technical skills and to study the way other artists have solved technical and artistic problems. Joining SIGGRAPH or ASIFA and talking to other professionals in your chosen field is also a way to further your education.

Below are some of the schools that have programs in animation or computer graphics and information about the two main professional organizations:

ANIMATION

Academy of Art College
Art Center College of Design
Art Institute of Chicago
California Institute of the Arts (CalArts)
New York University
Parsons School of Design
Pratt Institute
Rhode Island School of Design
Ringling School of Art and Design
Rochester Institute of Technology
San Francisco State University
Savannah College of Art and Design
School of Communication Arts
School of Visual Arts
Sheridan College
University of California, Los Angeles
University of Southern California
Vancouver Film School
Vancouver Institute of Media Arts

COMPUTER GRAPHICS

Art Institute of Chicago
Brown University

California Institute of Technology
California State University, Irvine
Carnegie-Mellon University
Cornell University
Massachusetts Institute of Technology
New York Institute of Technology
Princeton University
Stanford University
Texas A&M
University of California at Berkeley
University of California at Davis
University of North Carolina
University of Pennsylvania
University of Southern California
University of Utah
University of Washington[15]

PROFESSIONAL ORGANIZATIONS

ASIFA: Association International du Film d'Animation. An international organization founded in 1960 to support the art of animation. There are branches around the world and in the United States. The group also publishes the magazine *ASIFA News*.

SIGGRAPH: Special Interest Group for Computer Graphics. An organization formed to promote the distribution of information on computer graphics and to establish a community interested in innovation in the fields of computer graphics and interactive techniques. SIGGRAPH holds an annual conference in different cities around the United States.

CHAPTER NOTES

CHAPTER 1. CREATING MOVEMENT

1. John Lasseter, "Tricks to Animating Characters with a Computer," 1994, <http://www.siggraph.org/education/materials/HyperGraph/animation/character_animation/principles/lasseter_s94.htm> (April 20, 2005).

2. Frank Thomas and Ollie Johnston, *Disney Animation: The Illusion of Life* (New York: Abbeville Press, 1981), p. 18.

3. Rita Street, *Computer Animation, A Whole New World: Groundbreaking Work from Today's Top Animation Studios* (Gloucester, Mass.: Rockport Publishers, 1994), p. 106.

4. Thomas and Johnston, p. 339.

5. Ibid., p. 47.

6. Chuck Jones, *Chuck Amuck: The Life and Times of an Animated Cartoonist* (New York: Farrar Straus Giroux, 1989), p. 145.

7. *Chuck Jones: Extremes & Inbetweens, A Life in Animation*, television documentary, directed by Margaret Selby, 2002.

8. Leonard Maltin, *Of Mice and Magic: A History of American Animated Cartoons* (New York: New American Library, 1980), p. 49.

9. Barbara Robertson, "The Big and the Sméagol," January 2004, <http://cgw.pennnet.com/articles/article_display.cfm?Section=ARCHI&C=Feat&ARTICLE_ID=196304&KEYWORDS=gollum&p=18> (July 19, 2005).

10. Jones, p. 49.

11. Lasseter.

12. Maltin, p. 61.

13. Lasseter.

CHAPTER 2. TRADITIONAL CEL ANIMATION: TWO APPROACHES

1. Chuck Jones, *Chuck Amuck: The Life and Times of an Animated Cartoonist* (New York: Farrar Straus Giroux, 1989), p. 180.

2. Charles Solomon, *Enchanted Drawings: The History of Animation* (New York: Wings Books, 1994), p. 73.

3. Richard Williams, *The Animator's Survival Kit* (London: Faber and Faber, 2001), p. 18.

4. Frank Thomas and Ollie Johnston, *Disney Animation: The Illusion of Life* (New York: Abbeville Press, 1981), p. 62.

5. Ibid., p. 35.

6. Solomon, p. 52.

7. Jerry Beck, *Animation Art: From Pencil to Pixel, The History of Cartoon, Anime & CGI* (New York: Harper Collins, 2004) p. 37.

8. Leonard Maltin, *Of Mice and Magic: A History of American Animated Cartoons* (New York: New American Library, 1980), p. 47.

9. Solomon, p. 59.

10. Ibid., p. 62.

11. Maltin, p. 53.

12. Solomon, p. 58.

13. Beck, p. 59.

14. Thomas and Johnston, p. 245.

15. Richard Rickitt, *Special Effects: The History and Technique* (New York: Billboard Books, 2000) p. 141.

16. Jones, p 13.

17. Maltin, p. 53.

18. John Grant, *Masters of Animation* (New York: Watson-Guptill, 2001), p. 8.

19. John Canemaker, *Tex Avery: The MGM Years, 1942–1955* (Atlanta, Kansas City, Mo.: Turner Publishing, 1996), p. 14.

20. Ibid.

21. Ibid., p. 15.

22. Ibid., p. 17.

23. "Norman McLaren, April 11, 1914, Stirling Scotland—January 26, 1987," Montréal," n.d. <http://www.nfb.ca/portraits/fiche.php?id=285&v=h&lg=en> (August 24, 2005).

24. Julius Wiedemann, ed., *Animation Now! Anima Mundi* (Koln, Los Angeles: Taschen, 2004) p. 86.

25. "Biography: Nick Park," n.d. <http://movies2.nytimes.com/gst/movies/fimography.html> (August 24, 2005).

26. "Jan Švankmajer: Alchemist of the Surreal," April 1, 1998, <http://www.ilumin.co.uk/svank/intro.html> (August 24, 2005).

Chapter 3. Computer-Generated Animation

1. *The Incredibles* Press Kit, Buena Vista Releasing, Burbank, Calif., p. 11.

2. Film shown at *The Animated Performance: Art Meets Technology*, presented by the Academy of Motion Picture Arts and Sciences. Science and Technology Council, Beverly Hills, July 29, 2005.

3. Ibid.

4. Wendy Hall, "Interview with Jan Švankmajer," *Animato*, July 1997, <http://www.illumin.co.uk/svank/biog/inter/hall.html> (August 24, 2005).

5. Harry McCracken, "Luxo Sr., An Interview with John Lasseter," *Animato #19*, Winter, 1990 <http://www.harrymccracken.com/luxo.htm> (September 1, 2005).

6. Sharon Knolle, "Drawing the Line," *Variety*, January 10, 2005.

7. Richard Rickitt, *Special Effects: The History and Technique* (New York: Billboard Books, 2000), p. 162.

8. John Peterson, "Pixar and Disney's Toy Story, presented by Rick Sayre, Ronen Barzel, Rich Quade and Hickel at SIGGRAPH 1995," November 28, 1995 <http://siliconvalley.siggraph.org/MeetingNotes/ToyStory.html> (June 18, 2005).

9. *The Animated Performance*.

10. Ibid.

11. *The Incredibles* press kit, p. 11.

12. Ibid., p. 14.

13. Knolle.

14. *The Incredibles* press kit, p. 16.

15. Knolle.

16. *The Incredibles* press kit, p. 18

17. Ibid., p. 16.

18. "Artists Corner," n.d., <http://www.pixar.com/ artistscorner> (June 6, 2005).

CHAPTER 4. VISUAL EFFECTS: THEN AND NOW

1. David S. Cohen, "Technical Breakthroughs," *Variety*, December 3, 2004, p. A2.

2. Richard Rickitt, *Special Effects: The History and Technique* (New York: Billboard Books, 2000), p. 136.

3. Erin Ailworth, "Armed and Exceedingly Dangerous," *Los Angeles Times*, July 25, 2004, p. E12.

4. Pascal Pinteau, *Special Effects: An Oral History; Interviews with 38 Masters Spanning 100 Years* (New York: Harry N. Abrams, 2004), p. 32.

5. Ibid., pp. 32–33.

6. Patricia King Hanson, ed., *American Film Institute Catalog of Feature Films, 1931–1940* (Berkeley: University of California Press, 1993), p. 1103.

7. Linwood G. Dunn, "Creating Film Magic for the Original 'King Kong,'" *American Cinematographer*, Volume 58, January, 1977, p. 64.

8. George Turner with Oliver Goldner, *Spawn of Skull Island* (Baltimore: Luminary Press, 2002), p. 105.

9. Alan Osbourne, "Father of Kong," *Cinema Papers*, April 1974, p. 24.

10. Rickitt, pp. 222–223.

11. Dunn, pp. 64–65.

12. Turner, p. 130.

13. Dunn, p. 67.

14. Turner, pp. 131–132.

15. Dunn. p. 70.

16. Osbourne, p. 22.

17. Gary Russell, *The Lord of the Rings: The Art of The Fellowship of the Ring* (Boston: Houghton Mifflin, 2002), p. 9.

18. Pinteau, p. 184.

19. Official *Lord of the Rings* Movie Site, n.d. <http://www.lordoftherings.net/> (July 25, 2005).

20. Ibid.

21. Pinteau, p. 181.

22. Official *Lord of the Rings* Movie Site.

23. Pinteau, p. 184.

24. Ibid., p. 181.

25. Barbara Robertson, "The Big and the Sméagol," January, 2004, <http://cgw.pennnet.com/articles/article_display.cfm?Section=ARCHI&C=

Feat&ARTICLE_ID=196304&KEYWORDS=gollum& p=18> (July 19, 2005).

26. David Frankel, "Technical Breakthroughs: Van Helsing," *Variety*, December 3, 2004, p. A4.

CHAPTER 5. ANIMATION AND VISUAL EFFECTS ON TELEVISION

1. Kit Laybourne, *The Animation Book: A Complete Guide to Animated Filmmaking—from Flipbooks to Sound Cartoons to 3-D Animation*, rev. ed. (New York: Three Rivers Press, 1998), p. 210.

2. Ibid., pp. 190–191.

3. Chris Turner, *Planet Simpson: How a Cartoon Masterpiece Defined a Generation* (Cambridge, Mass: DaCapo Press, 2004) p. 15.

4. Turner, pp. 35–36.

5. Ibid., p. 24.

6. Ibid.

7. Nancy Cartwright, *My Life as a Ten-Year-Old Boy* (New York: Hyperion, 2000), p. 106.

8. Turner, p. 23.

9. Cartwright, pp. 125–130.

10. Ibid., p. 202.

11. Ibid., p. 214.

12. Jerry Beck, *Animation Art: From Pencil to Pixel* (New York: Harper Collins, 2004) p. 313.

13. "Q&A with Al Jean: Executive Producer, *The Simpsons*," <http://www.tkukoulu.fi/~kerttuli/netdays2002/qa.html> (September 1, 2005).

14. Cartwright, p. 223.

15. Jon Burlingame, "'Lost' Art of Real Players: Music-minded Voters Favor Series that Use Live Musicians for Tracks," *Variety*, August 18, 2005, p. A2.

16. Turner, p. 39.

17. David Carr, "Will The Simpsons Ever Age?" *The New York Times*, April 24, 2005, p. 22.

18. Stuart Levine, "Practical Magic: Invisible F/X Proliferate in Primetime," *Variety*, July 27, 2005, p. A4.

19. Eric A. Taub, "Special (and Mundane) Effects of the Movies, on TV," *New York Times*, May 12, 2003.

20. Ibid.

21. Levine.

22. John Grant, *Masters of Animation* (New York: Watson-Guptill, 2001), p. 177.

23. Dimitra Geogakis, "Radium: Radium Creates Magic for Hip Hop's Leading Lady," n.d., <http://usa.autodesk.com> (September 5, 2005).

24. Alan Citron and Daniel Cerone, "There Are No Limits in Michael Jackson's World of Make-Believe," *Los Angeles Times*, November 14, 1991, p. F1.

25. Matthew Armstrong "Music Videos: Shrinking Budgets and Long Hours Don't Scare Post Pros Away From These 'Short Films,'" November 2004, <http://www.findarticles.com/p/articles/mi_m0HNN/is_11_19/ai_n8575088> (September 9, 2005).

26. Anne Thompson, "FX Gods: The 10 Visual Effects of Artists Who Rule Hollywood," *Wired Magazine*, February, 2005, <http://www.wired.com/wired/archive/13.02/fxgods.html> (February 8, 2005).

27. Ibid.

28. Pascal Pinteau, *Special Effects: An Oral History; Interviews with 38 Masters Spanning 100 Years* (New York: Harry N. Abrams, 2004), p. 458.

29. Pinteau, p. 526.

30. Piers Bizony, *Digital Domain: The Leading Edge of Visual Effects* (New York: Billboard Books, 2001), p. 248.

31. Universal Studios Amusement Park, n.d. <http://themeparks.universalstudios.com/hollywood/website/attr_mummy.html> (August 10, 2005).

32. Universal Studios Amusement Park, n.d. <http://themeparks.universalstudios.com/hollywood/website/shrek.htmlfeatures3-D.html> (August 10, 2005).

Chapter 6. Careers in Animation and Visual Effects

1. Jerry Beck, *Animation Art: From Pencil to Pixel, The History of Cartoon, Anime & CGI* (New York: Harper Collins, 2004), p. 9

2. Harry McCracken, "Luxo Sr., An Interview with John Lasseter," *Animato #19*, Winter, 1990, <http://www.harrymccracken.com/luxo.htm> (September 1, 2005).

3. Ron Magid, "2005 Next Gen," *The Hollywood Reporter*, February 16, 2005. p. 26.

4. Sean Elder, "Is TV the Coolest Invention Ever Invented? Subversive Cartoonist Matt Groening Goes Prime Time," *Mother Jones*, December 1989, p. 31.

5. Chuck Jones, *Chuck Amuck: The Life and Times of an Animated Cartoonist* (New York: Farrar Straus Giroux, 1989), p. 55.

6. McCracken.

7. Ibid.

8. "Pixar Artist's Corner—Steve," 2005. <http://www.pixar.com/artistscorner/steve/index.html> (June 6, 2005).

9. Les Chappell, "'Lord of the Rings' Visual Effects Creator Talks About Entrepreneurial Experiences," June 7, 2004, <http://wistechnology.com/article.php?id=899> (July 6, 2005).

10. "So You Want to Be in Pixels: Ellen Poon," n.d., <www.pbs.org/wgbh/nova/specialfx2/poon.html> (July 6, 2005).

11. Anne Thompson, "FX Gods: The 10 Visual Effects Artists Who Rule Hollywood," *Wired Magazine*, February, 2005, <http://www.wired.com/wired/archive/13.02/fxgods.html> (February 8, 2005).

12. Kara Lynch, "Lyndon Barrois: Master of the Matrix," n.d., <http://www.blackfilmmakermag.com/asp/features.asp> (August 30, 2005).

13. Aardman Animations Ltd., 2004, <http://www.aardman.com> (August 15, 2005).

14. Lev Grossman, "How to Get Famous in 30 Seconds," *TIME*, April 24, 2006, p. 66.

15. "Pixar Jobs-Schools," 2005, <http://www.pixar.com/companyinfo/jobs/schools.html> (June 6, 2005).

GLOSSARY

animatics—A film, video, or computer compilation of animators' drawings that allows them to refine sequences before they are actually animated.

animation—The process of photographing models, puppets, pictures, or artwork one frame at a time.

animatronic—A remote-controlled system that uses mechanical devices to produce a life-like performance using puppets or models.

anticipation—An animation technique in which a character indicates a major action before it begins.

armature—The underlying framework or skeleton of a model or puppet.

audio-animatronics—Animatronics with synchronized voice tracks.

avars—Animated variables that computer animators use to control and change elements of the models.

blue screen process—An optical process by which subjects filmed in front of a blue screen are combined with a separately filmed background.

cel—A transparent sheet of plastic used in hand-drawn animation.

cel animation—The traditional method of creating hand-drawn two-dimensional animation. Each frame is drawn and painted on a clear acetate cel.

character animation—Animation that reveals a character's personality by the way it moves and behaves.

clay animation—A form of animation in which the figures to be animated are sculpted out of modeling clay and put into motion one frame or movement at a time. Animator Will Vinton dubbed this process "claymation."

close up—When a character or object is drawn or photographed from a short distance.

compositing—A method of blending separate visual components into one shot.

computer graphics (CG)—Any two- or three-dimensional image created entirely within a computer. Also called CGI (computer-generated imagery).

cycles—A method of animating in which an action such as walking takes place in a continuous loop.

digital—Recording, storing, and transmitting images, sounds, and data in the computer in combinations of ones and zeros. Digital information can be copied and transmitted repeatedly with no loss of detail.

extremes—The beginning and ending drawings of an animated movement.

follow through—The extension and continuation of an animated action.

frame—A single image on a film strip.

genre—A category or type of story.

in-betweens—The stages of action between key frames.

key drawings—The drawings that indicate story points or major changes, or that tell what is happening in the scene. In computer generated animation they are called key frames.

limited cel animation—Animation drawn on the smallest number of cels possible.

long shot—Describes a film shot when a character or object is shown at a distance and appears small in the frame.

matte—Something used to mask off a selected area of the camera's field of view.

matte painting—A large painting used to depict backgrounds too costly to create or find.

miniature—Any object or location that is reproduced at a smaller than life-size scale for filming purposes.

miniature rear projection—Projection of filmed live action onto small screens erected in miniature sets.

model—Any object or location that has been reproduced for filming purposes.

morphing—A process that makes one image appear to transform seamlessly into another.

motion capture—Also called performance capture. A method of capturing the natural movement

121

of bodies or faces so that it can be used for animating computer-generated characters.

optical effects—All effects that are not done physically but are made using cameras, computers, and other technology.

overlapping action—In animating figures and objects, different parts of the animation move separately from each other.

pencil test—A film of animated sketches made to test animation before it is transferred to cels.

persistence of vision—The illusion of movement created when a series of still pictures flashes by in rapid succession.

perspective—A technique in drawing and painting in which parallel lines are represented as converging so as to give the illusion of depth and distance.

pixels—An abbreviation of "picture element." Pixels are the tiny squares of color that make up a digital image. Each image consists of many thousands of pixels.

pixilation—Using a technique similar to stop-motion animation, a camera is set to film live action performance at regular intervals. The result is speeded up action that makes the actors seem to float or fly.

prosthetics—False limbs, noses, or other appendages that are attached to the face or body of a performer.

rear projection—A method of combining live-action foregrounds with pre-filmed background scenery.

registration device—Any device that keeps an animator's drawings lined up exactly.

render—Translating the information that makes up a movie from digital data into actual frames of film.

rotoscope—A method of projecting live action footage so that it can be traced frame by frame by an animator.

secondary action—An action that takes place after a character's main action.

slow motion—An effect that makes action appear unnaturally slow.

special effects animation—The animation of any moving object or substance other than the main characters, such as water, falling leaves, fire, smoke, clouds, and shadows.

sprocket holes—Small perforations along the edges of a film strip that hook on to the teeth of a sprocket wheel and move the film through a camera or projector.

squash and stretch—Extreme positions in an animated movement. Squash and stretch can be exaggerated for comic effect.

stop-motion—A method of animating models by physically altering their position in between the photography of each frame.

storyboard—A device, similar to a comic strip or graphic novel, that is used to plan animated films.

subsurface scattering—Describes what happens when light strikes a translucent surface, spreads inside the material, and then is either absorbed or leaves the surface from a different point.

three dimensional (3-D)—Traditional cartoon animation is two-dimensional, showing only height and width. Model, or stop-motion animation, is three-dimensional, showing height, width, and depth. The camera and the models can move in all dimensions during animation.

timing—The number of drawings it takes to complete an action. The more drawings, the longer the action lasts on screen and the smoother the action appears.

traveling matte—Traveling mattes are used to combine two separately filmed elements when the foreground element (a person, for example) changes shape or position from frame to frame, necessitating a new matte for each frame. Today, most traveling mattes are created digitally.

virtual camera—The hypothetical camera used to film animation and environments created within the computer. It is not actually a camera but rather the "device" used to describe the viewpoint that the computer will use.

FURTHER READING

Books

Hamilton, Jake. *Special Effects.* New York: Dorling Kindersley Publishing, 1998.

Kerlow, Isaac Victor. *The Art of 3-D Computer Animation and Effects*. New York: John Wiley & Sons, 2003.

Vince, John. *Essential Computer Animation Fast: How to Understand the Techniques and Potential of Computer Animation*. New York: Springer, 2000.

Internet Addresses

Animation World Network
http://www.awn.com/

Animation Career Information
http://www.adigitaldreamer.com/articles/ animationcareerinfo.htm

How to Get Started in a Special Effects Career
http://ct.essortment.com/specialeffects_rgyq.htm

INDEX